BARRON'S BOOK NOTES

WILLIAM SHAKESPEARE'S

Twelfth Night

BARRON'S BOOK NOTES

WILLIAM SHAKESPEARE'S

Twelfth Night

BY

Robert Owens Scott

ASSOCIATE PRODUCER
Playhouse Repertory Company
New York City

SERIES COORDINATOR
Murray Bromberg
Principal, Wang High School of Queens
Holliswood, New York

BARRON'S

BARRON'S EDUCATIONAL SERIES, INC.
Woodbury, New York • London • Toronto • Sydney

ACKNOWLEDGMENTS

Our thanks to Milton Katz and Julius Liebb for their contribution to the Book Notes series.

Loreto Todd, Senior Lecturer in English, University of Leeds, England, prepared the chapter on Elizabethan English in this book.

All inquiries should be addressed to:
Barron's Educational Series, Inc.
113 Crossways Park Drive
Woodbury, New York 11797

Library of Congress Catalog Card No. 85-1389

International Standard Book No. 0-8120-3548-8

Library of Congress Cataloging in Publication Data

Scott, Robert Owens.
  William Shakespeare's Twelfth night.

  (Barron's book notes)
  Bibliography: p. 110
  Summary: A guide to reading "Twelfth Night" with a
critical and appreciative mind. Includes background on
the author's life and times, sample tests, term paper
suggestions, and a reading list.
    1. Shakespeare, William, 1564–1616. Twelfth night.
  [1. Shakespeare, William, 1564–1616. Twelfth night.
  2. English literature—History and criticism]
  I. Title. II. Series.
PR2837.S36 1985   822.3'3   85-1389
ISBN 0-8120-3548-8

PRINTED IN THE UNITED STATES OF AMERICA

567   550   987654321

CONTENTS

ADVISORY BOARD

HOW TO USE THIS BOOK

You have to know how to approach literature in order to get the most out of it. This *Barron's Book Notes* volume follows a plan based on methods used by some of the best students to read a work of literature.

Begin with the guide's section on the author's life and times. As you read, try to form a clear picture of the author's personality, circumstances, and motives for writing the work. This background usually will make it easier for you to hear the author's tone of voice, and follow where the author is heading.

Then go over the rest of the introductory material—such sections as those on the plot, characters, setting, themes, and style of the work. Underline, or write down in your notebook, particular things to watch for, such as contrasts between characters and repeated literary devices. At this point, you may want to develop a system of symbols to use in marking your text as you read. (Of course, you should only mark up a book you own, not one that belongs to another person or a school.) Perhaps you will want to use a different letter for each character's name, a different number for each major theme of the book, a different color for each important symbol or literary device. Be prepared to mark up the pages of your book as you read. Put your marks in the margins so you can find them again easily.

Now comes the moment you've been waiting for—the time to start reading the work of literature. You may want to put aside your *Barron's Book Notes* volume until you've read the work all the way through. Or you may want to alternate, reading the *Book Notes* analysis of each section as soon as you have finished reading the corresponding part of the original. Before you move on, reread crucial passages you don't fully understand. (Don't take this guide's analysis for granted—make up your own mind as to what the work means.)

Once you've finished the whole work of literature, you may want to review it right away, so you can firm up your ideas about what it means. You may want to leaf through the book concentrating on passages you marked in reference to one character or one theme. This is also a good time to reread the *Book Notes* introductory material, which pulls together insights on specific topics.

When it comes time to prepare for a test or to write a paper, you'll already have formed ideas about the work. You'll be able to go back through it, refreshing your memory as to the author's exact words and perspective, so that you can support your opinions with evidence drawn straight from the work. Patterns will emerge, and ideas will fall into place; your essay question or term paper will almost write itself. Give yourself a dry run with one of the sample tests in the guide. These tests present both multiple-choice and essay questions. An accompanying section gives answers to the multiple-choice questions as well as suggestions for writing the essays. If you have to select a term paper topic, you may choose one from the list of suggestions in this book. This guide also provides you with a reading list, to help you when you start research for a term paper, and a selection of provocative comments by critics, to spark your thinking before you write.

THE AUTHOR AND HIS TIMES

It is lucky for us that William Shakespeare lived in a time of ferment like the Renaissance. In another time, this grandson of tenant farmers who never went to a university might not have had the opportunity to become a playwright. During the Renaissance, England was a place of change and opportunity. The discovery of the New World brought excitement and wealth. The old feudal order was passing away. Though the structure of society was still strictly divided into classes, some movement between the ranks became possible.

Shakespeare grew up in the small town of Stratford. His father, John Shakespeare, was a merchant and glovemaker. By the time of William's birth in 1564, John was doing well. He had married Mary Arden, the daughter of a well-to-do landowner, and had held several important offices in the local government. No records exist to prove the exact date of William's birth, but we know he was baptized on April 26, 1564. Because most infants were baptized when they were three days old, April 23 is traditionally considered Shakespeare's birthday.

After 1577, John apparently came upon financial hard times. His name disappeared from the list of town councillors and was entered on the record of those *not* seen attending church. Most likely, he was in debt.

Shakespeare probably attended the free grammar school in Stratford, where he could have received a good education, and a thorough grounding in the Latin classics. No further official documentation of his activities exists until his marriage contract with Anne Hathaway, signed on November 28, 1582. Anne was older than William by eight years. Their first child, Susanna, was born in May, 1583. In 1585, Anne gave birth to twins—Judith and Hamnet.

We don't know how Shakespeare made his living in Stratford. He may have been a schoolteacher or a private tutor. Tradition has it that he had to leave Stratford because he was caught poaching. More likely he went to London in search of opportunity.

Whatever reason Shakespeare may have had for leaving his home town, opportunity was clearly what he found in London. The next surviving public document to mention his name is a pamphlet written by playwright Robert Greene in 1592. By that time, Shakespeare had arrived in London and become an actor. What's more, he had begun writing plays. Greene condescendingly refers to Shakespeare as an upstart actor who has the nerve to think he can write as well as an educated gentleman. If the venom of Greene's attack is a measure of envy, Shakespeare must have been doing well by then.

The fact that a man who had never been to a university presumed to write plays probably offended Greene's sense of order and propriety. He was not the only one made uncomfortable by the changes in the social order brought about by the Renaissance. Change always brings with it a certain amount of resentment, especially among those people who were happy with the status quo.

Twelfth Night was not written as a social treatise, and it would be a serious mistake to try to make it one. Nonetheless, in the Illyria of the play you find a society that has much in common with Shakespeare's London.

The modern idea of equality had no place in Elizabethan thinking. No one doubted that some people were better than others. There was a definite hierarchy, an order in society. Philosophically, this reflected the order in the universe. When people behaved improperly, either by pretending to be better than they were or by failing to live up to the standards expected of them, the whole world would become disordered. In *Twelfth Night*, part of the comic disorder is caused by the aspirations of Malvolio and Sir Andrew, and by the emotional self-indulgence of Orsino and Olivia.

Orsino and Olivia are important in the world of Illyria because they are at the top of this social ladder. They are the nobles, and are expected to behave nobly. Rank definitely had its privileges, but it had duties as well. Those duties included behaving suitably and sensibly.

Two of the other characters in *Twelfth Night*, Sir Andrew Aguecheek and Sir Toby Belch, belong to the same class as Orsino and Olivia, though they are at the bottom end of it. Their failures are far more extreme than those of Olivia and Orsino, and so they are more ludicrously comic.

Some readers see them as representatives of knighthood in decline. We cannot help but notice that Sir Andrew seems completely untrained in the skills a knight should have. Instead, there is a great fuss about his wealth. This provides a bit of social satire. In Shakespeare's day, a man with enough money could buy a knighthood. (Queen Elizabeth

I was known to sell even higher titles on occasion.) You can imagine that the members of the older aristocracy were less than thrilled to have their ranks invaded by these wealthy upstarts. If Sir Andrew's knighthood comes from wealth and not from birth, it is utterly ridiculous for him to hope to marry someone as high above him as Olivia.

Below these characters are the servants, the lower class. If they had little in the way of rights, they also had little in the way of obligations. Therefore, they are far freer to indulge in foolishness of one sort or another, and these are the characters who are likely to be involved in scenes of slapstick comedy.

This class was not, however, immune to the virus of social climbing. In *Twelfth Night*, you can see this in the character of the Puritan steward Malvolio.

Missing from the play, but growing in reality in Shakespeare's time, is the middle class. This class, to which Shakespeare himself belonged, did not appear too much in literature yet. Stories tended to reflect the society of a somewhat earlier world.

Moving freely among all the classes, both in the play and in real life, was the fool. Most royal and many noble households kept a fool (or clown) for entertainment. This was the court jester, a term you may have heard. Natural fools were actual idiots, kept for amusement. Wise fools, like Feste in this play, were intelligent and witty.

Court fools occupied a special place in society. They could move back and forth from the kitchen to the king's chamber. Some even accompanied their noble employers on state occasions. Frequently they were allowed far more license of speech than would be permitted anyone else.

Although the idea of hierarchy, of an order in nature reflected in the social order, was generally accepted in Shakespeare's time, society was actually far more flexible than it had been, and change could be seen everywhere. One change that can be seen in *Twelfth Night* is in the attitude toward romantic Courtly Love.

Popularized by the medieval troubadors, the point of Courtly Love was that it was never consummated. The lover devoted himself to a beloved who, for some reason, could never be his. What was important was the exquisite suffering of the lover as he dedicated himself to the unobtainable.

In *Twelfth Night*, Orsino obviously sees himself as a courtly lover. Olivia as well, in her extravagant devotion to her dead brother, is indulging herself in romantic notions. In contrast are Viola and Sebastian, the honest and practical brother and sister.

Shakespeare was already an extremely popular playwright when *Twelfth Night* was first performed about 1600, and his success continued. His works after *Twelfth Night* include the four great tragedies—*Hamlet*, *Othello*, *King Lear*, and *Macbeth*. In 1603, Shakespeare's company was chartered by Elizabeth's successor, James I, as the King's Men. When Shakespeare retired to Stratford in 1611, he lived in the second biggest house in town, called New Place. On April 23 (possibly the same day of the year on which he was born) in 1616, he died.

THE PLAY

The Plot

Orsino, the duke of Illyria, is helplessly in love with the Countess Olivia. She, however, refuses to return his affections, preferring instead to mourn her dead brother. She will not even see the messengers he sends daily. Rejection only seems to increase Orsino's ardor. He spends his days listening to sad music and pining away for Olivia.

A shipwreck throws a stranger, Viola, a young woman of noble birth, onto the shore of Illyria and into the middle of this situation. She believes her brother was drowned in the same shipwreck. Needing some time to get her bearings in this strange country, she disguises herself as a boy, calls herself Cesario, and presents herself to Duke Orsino. He immediately takes a liking to this "boy" and sends "him" as a messenger to Olivia. Viola/Cesario does what Orsino asks, but she has a problem—she has fallen in love with Orsino herself!

Viola/Cesario proves to be an excellent messenger when she calls on Olivia. Her determination wins her an audience with the lady. She movingly pleads Orsino's case. Olivia resists the entreaties on Orsino's behalf. When Viola/Cesario leaves, however, you learn the truth. Olivia has now fallen hopelessly in love with Viola/Cesario! She sends her puritanical steward Malvolio after Viola/Cesario with a ring.

Malvolio rudely accosts Viola/Cesario and repeats the lie Olivia told him—that the ring was a gift from Orsino and that Olivia is returning it. Viola/Cesario knows that she gave the lady no ring. She quickly figures out the truth. Olivia is in love with somebody who doesn't exist.

Meanwhile, Olivia has another suitors, Sir Andrew Aguecheek, a simpleton who fancies himself a ladies' man. The wealthy Aguecheek is being deceived by Olivia's uncle, Sir Toby Belch, into believing he has a chance of winning Olivia's hand. Actually, Sir Toby is toying with Sir Andrew, milking him for his money. They live in Olivia's house and spend all night drinking and carousing.

Sir Toby and Malvolio are natural enemies. Toby hates propriety, while Malvolio always assumes a solemn manner. Actually, the self-righteous Malvolio harbors the mad hope that his lady Olivia will one day marry him and make him her equal. Olivia's maid Maria scolds Sir Toby for his rude ways, but she has a touch of mischief in her, too. It is she who invents the plot to get revenge on Malvolio.

The plot works like this: Maria forges a letter from Olivia to her "secret love." Then, she leaves it where Malvolio will find it. Malvolio, in his egotism, believes the letter is meant for him. He follows its ridiculous instructions—to wear yellow stockings, smile constantly and be "opposite with a kinsman, surly with servants." When he behaves that way in front of Olivia, she is convinced he has gone crazy and has him locked away.

Sir Andrew sees Olivia trying to woo "Cesario." Egged on by Sir Toby, he challenges Viola/Cesario to a duel. Viola/Cesario, who is in fact a girl, and

Sir Andrew, who is really a coward, are both ma-
nipulated by Sir Toby. Sir Toby enjoys terrifying
both of them by convincing each that the other is
a great duelist who has killed many men.

Fate plays its own joke, however, when Viola/
Cesario's twin brother Sebastian arrives in Illyria.
Sebastian believes that his sister was drowned in
the shipwreck. He's confused when Olivia accosts
him and demands that he marry her (she thinks
he is Cesario). Olivia is surprised herself when he
agrees. She quickly gets him to repeat his promise
in front of a priest.

The numerous confusions all come to a head and
then unravel when Orsino calls upon Olivia. She
says that Viola/Cesario has promised to marry her.
Viola/Cesario denies it. The priest confirms Olivia's story. Both Orsino and Olivia believe they
have been betrayed. Just then, Sir Andrew and Sir
Toby come in, beaten and bleeding. Sir Andrew
claims that they have been fighting with Viola/Ce-
sario. He is surprised to see his enemy there before
him.

It was Sebastian, of course, who gave them their
beating. His entrance shocks Orsino, Olivia, and
the others, who think they must be going crazy.
Viola, however, is overjoyed to be reunited with
the brother she thought was dead. She reveals that
she is a woman.

The confusion dispelled, things quickly fall into
their natural order. Orsino marries Viola. Olivia
marries Sebastian. Sir Toby marries the witty Maria.
Only Malvolio clings to his self-love, refuses to accept the apology he is offered, and stalks off, vowing revenge on everybody.

The Characters

Viola

In the middle of the group of outrageous characters who inhabit the world of *Twelfth Night* stands one of Shakespeare's most level-headed creations. It may seem odd to us that circumstances should force Viola to disguise herself as a boy, but she reacts to people and situations in a way you can understand and identify with.

Viola is young, beautiful, and nobly born. These qualities you hear about from the other characters. She is also extremely smart and deeply passionate. These qualities can be seen in what she does.

Her intelligence takes two forms. First, see how skillfully she chooses her words when she wants to tell Orsino she loves him. Her passion drives her to tell him how she feels. Still, she must not let him guess that she is a girl. Therefore, her statements have to sound plausible coming from Cesario. Or look at her scenes with Olivia. In Act I, Scene v, Viola can play any word game Olivia wishes to indulge in. Viola displays as much skill with words as any lawyer or scholar.

The other kind of intelligence Viola possesses is an instinctive sense of how to take care of herself. She knows the danger she could be in as a young girl alone in a strange place. That's why she adopts the disguise of a young boy. She puts herself in a position where she can rely on her own quick wits.

Her passion is revealed in the way she expresses herself. Since she cannot simply turn to Orsino and say "I love you," the intensity of her feelings is reflected in the poetry of her speech. One of the best and most famous examples is the passage in Act II, Scene iv where she tells Orsino about the love her "sister" had to conceal. (Of course, Viola is really talking about her own feelings.) Another example is in Act I, Scene v. Disguised as Cesario, Viola tells what she would do to woo Olivia if she were Orsino. Olivia is moved so deeply that she falls in love with "Cesario"!

The love Viola feels is sincere and mature. She puts Orsino's happiness before her own. He loves Olivia, so Viola woos the lady for him.

Viola is patient and optimistic. She faces her impossible situation with relative calm. Time, she says, must sort out these problems. The other characters get into trouble by trying to provide their own answers. In the end, Viola's patience is rewarded.

Although she wears a disguise, and in that sense is presenting a false face to the world, Viola can actually be considered the most honest character in the play.

Orsino

Like several other characters in this play, Orsino doesn't understand himself. He sees himself as a man smitten by a woman—Olivia. Of all the lovers who have ever lived, he thinks that he is the most sincere and ardent. In truth, he is in love with love. Olivia is the nominal object of his affections, but he is obsessed with love itself.

Orsino's wooing of Olivia seems unreal. Until the very end of the play, he never tries to see the lady himself. Instead, he sends messengers. Also, Olivia has clearly and repeatedly stated that she does not love him. He has no reason to believe her attitude will ever change. He seems to admire his own emotions more than he admires Olivia.

The play suggests that Orsino craves the melancholy feeling that comes from unrequited love. His favorite song tells the story of a man who suffered so terribly when his lady rejected him that he killed himself!

As the wealthy and powerful duke of Illyria, Orsino can spend his time any way he chooses. What he chooses is to lie about, listen to music, and talk about how wonderful love is. Once Viola (disguised as Cesario) becomes part of his household, he talks with the "boy" about love. Olivia rarely gets mentioned. Love alone is "high fantastical," he says in Act I. Accordingly, he seems never to think about anything else.

Some readers wonder how Viola could love such a self-indulgent person. Perhaps she sees that, though he is self-deceived, he is completely sincere. Orsino simply cannot see beyond his own obsession. And you know from what the sea captain says in Act I, Scene ii, that Orsino is regarded as a noble gentleman. He speaks like a man of charm and intelligence.

In the end, Orsino comes to his senses. Once he discovers that "Cesario" is actually Viola, the fact that Olivia doesn't want him becomes unimportant. To his credit, he immediately realizes that Viola is the proper mate for him. The comic foolishness of his previous insistence on marrying Olivia is quickly forgiven and forgotten.

Though Orsino's love-sick behavior is humorous, he is no silly caricature. In fact he is deeply human. Those who have ached with an intense longing for the love of some unattainable person can emphathize with him. Have you ever nursed an unrealistic crush or infatuation for somebody who may not have even known you were alive? Later, you may look back and laugh, saying "I certainly was silly," but at the time the feeling was both painful and wonderful. Orsino's condition is a common one, and books, plays, and movies are filled with similar characters. Orsino's behavior is theatrically exaggerated, and therefore funny. At the same time it is recognizably human, and therefore touching.

Olivia

Olivia resembles Orsino in several ways. Like the duke, she is wealthy, attractive, and nobly born. She rules her large household firmly but kindly. Olivia and Orsino would seem to be a good match. But the lady's resoluteness in refusing Orsino's love equals his determination to have her.

Her tendency toward excess is just as strong as Orsino's. Her wealth allows her to do whatever she wants. At the beginning of the play, she has announced that she intends to mourn her dead brother for no less than seven years. Then, after meeting Cesario (really Viola in disguise), she cannot think about anything but the boy and how much she wants to marry him.

Some readers interpret her proposal to mourn her brother for seven years as a ploy to get attention. Compare her behavior with Viola's. Does Viola love her brother less? The play never says why Olivia has decided to mourn for so long. Perhaps she would like to think of herself as the kind of person who suffers greatly. It could be that the lady herself doesn't know. As Olivia says when she falls in love with Cesario, people frequently are driven by feelings and desires they do not understand. Most of the characters in the play don't understand themselves any better than Olivia does.

Unlike Orsino, Olivia pursues the one she loves directly. She constantly tries to win the boy's heart. His refusal frustrates her. At times it makes her angry. She knows that what she does is neither wise nor dignified. Still, she never gives up.

Olivia's nature is compassionate. Though Sir Toby Belch's rude ways must offend her sensibilities, she takes good care of him. She will not allow her steward Malvolio to make fun of Feste. Later, when Malvolio has been humiliated, she feels genuinely sorry for him.

Olivia has a quick mind. She can trade quips with the fool and verbally spar with Viola. The verbal facility of both ladies makes their scenes (Act I, Scene v and Act III, Scene i) especially enjoyable.

She is also a good judge of character. She knows that Malvolio is "sick of self love." She also knows that her uncle, Sir Toby, is a drunk. Olivia can even assess Orsino's character accurately. She says that he is noble, wealthy, smart, and brave, and that his only problem is he insists that he loves a lady who will not have him.

Why does such a shrewd woman make a bad mistake when she falls in love? From what Olivia says at the end of Act I, Scene v, she doesn't know the reason herself. Many readers blame it on her impulsiveness. Cesario makes a strong impression on her, so she immediately gives him her heart. Other readers feel that Viola's passionate plea in her master's behalf wins the lady's heart. What-

ever Olivia's motivation may be, her behavior helps
to make clear that love can make otherwise rational
people act in an irrational fashion.

Malvolio

Malvolio belongs to the servant class. As Olivia's
steward, he has a place near the seat of power in
the household. He would like nothing better than
to wield that power himself. In his heart, he firmly
believes that he is better than those he serves. It
seems to him that Olivia treats him with special
respect. Perhaps he misunderstands her kindness
because he himself would not be kind to those
below him. His name suggests "ill will." When his
lady is not around, Malvolio takes it upon himself
to try to discipline others, even, at times, his social
superiors, like Sir Toby. Most of the time, Olivia
seems to appreciate the solemn dignity with which
he carries out his duties. The others, however, sense
his arrogant attitude and regard him as an enemy.

Malvolio is actually in disguise. He pretends to
be a Puritan. He dresses in black. Nothing amuses
him. Nobody ever sees him smile. But this is merely
a pose he assumes, one that allows him to criticize
others.

Under his black garments beats a heart filled with
vanity. His daydreams all have to do with the time
when Olivia will make him her equal by marrying
him. He sees himself wearing fine clothes and jew-
elry. The household would then be his to command. He could get revenge on those who haven't
treated him respectfully.

It is ironic that Malvolio is much more successful
at fooling himself than he is at deceiving others.
The other members of the household all see that

he is a prig and a hypocrite. Even Olivia, who seems to value him as a servant, says he is "sick of self love" (*Act I, Scene i, line 92*).

Though others can see through him, Malvolio fools himself completely. As Maria says, he believes that "all that look on him love him" (*Act II, Scene iii, line 152*). He is sure that only some accident of luck caused such a fine man as himself to be born a servant rather than a master. Fortune, he thinks, will eventually correct its mistake.

Malvolio's self deception makes him the perfect target for Maria and Sir Toby's joke. Maria's letter is only able to convince him that Olivia loves him because that's what he wants to believe. When the letter tells him to act proud and haughty, it only gives him permission to show how he already feels. His own pride causes him to act as foolishly as he does.

But Malvolio's real downfall is not caused by foolishness. Nearly everybody in this play is foolish at one time or another. Unlike the others, however, Malvolio simply cannot laugh at himself, cannot recognize his own faults. Therefore, he has no part in the healing that occurs at the end of the play. While the others are all laughing at themselves and forgiving each other, Malvolio clings to his anger. When he makes his final exit, he vows to take revenge on everybody. Does he have an excuse? Did the joke go too far? Or were the others justified in trying to take him down a peg or two?

Sir Toby Belch

Sir Toby Belch, like Malvolio, lives up to the sound of his name. He spends every night and most days getting drunk. As Olivia's uncle, Sir

Toby has the run of the house. Taking advantage of her generosity, he concerns himself primarily with eating and drinking, and seems completely unconcerned with what anybody thinks of him. Even when he tries to behave properly around his niece, he usually fails. He cannot conceal how drunk he is.

Sir Toby has a practical side. At least he watches out for his own interests. His main drinking companion is Sir Andrew Aguecheek. Though it's obvious Sir Andrew is a dim-witted fool, he has a value for Sir Toby. Sir Andrew is a rich fool, and Sir Toby manipulates him well. Whenever Sir Toby needs money, Sir Andrew sends home for some.

In fact, Sir Toby is extremely clever. Look at his first scene with Maria (*Act II, Scene iii*). He plays with the meaning of everything she says in a very sophisticated manner. What he's doing is deflecting criticism that he does not want to hear.

Sir Toby is also a shrewd judge of character. For example, he knows exactly how much Olivia will let him get away with. He can tell that Maria loves him from the way she treats him, though she has probably never told him so. He can predict what Sir Andrew will do with complete accuracy.

All this adds up to a description of a thoroughly selfish character. But is that all there is to him? What most readers enjoy about Sir Toby is his sense of fun. His philosophy seems to be that life is to be lived and enjoyed. He doesn't mind what others do as long as they leave him alone to enjoy himself.

Therefore, there is nobody Sir Toby hates more

than a killjoy like Malvolio. His most famous line sums up his attitude. When Malvolio scolds Sir Toby and his friends for being up late drinking, Sir Toby responds, "Dost thou think, because thou art virtuous, there shall be no more cakes and ale?" (*Act II, Scene iii, lines 117–118*). Malvolio can be as much of a prig as he wants to be, for all Sir Toby cares. He just should not try to interfere with other people's pleasures.

By the end of the play, Sir Toby has been both punished and rewarded. For carrying one of his practical jokes too far, he gets a good beating. That humiliation is enough to make up for his sins, however. Fabian reports later (*Act V, Scene i, line 391*) that Maria and Sir Toby have been married. Though Sir Toby clearly has not "reformed," he is allowed to share in the happy ending.

Sir Andrew Aguecheek

In Sir Andrew Aguecheek, Shakespeare creates a "natural" fool. Unlike Feste, who is a wise fool, Sir Andrew is entertaining in spite of himself. Though he is vain and often arrogant, you cannot hate him. Unlike Malvolio, he is not malicious. He causes no real harm. If you stop laughing at his antics for a moment, you are likely to pity him. He never quite catches on to what is going on around him. He places his trust in Sir Toby who befriends him only because he is rich. Sir Toby deceives him into thinking that he has a chance of winning Olivia's hand. In Sir Andrew, Sir Toby has a willing dupe.

Poor Sir Andrew spends his energy trying to live up to the false picture he has of himself. As a knight, he believes he should be skilled in all the courtly virtues. He claims to be a good dancer, but his attempts to execute even the simplest steps are laughable. A courtier should speak different languages. Sir Andrew only makes a fool of himself when he tries to use the few phrases of French he has managed to learn.

Sir Andrew is easily led by others, especially by Sir Toby. Sir Andrew adores Sir Toby, who helps him believe he really is what he would like to be. It's amusing to watch Sir Toby manipulate the knight. No resolution of Sir Andrew's is so strong that Sir Toby cannot completely turn him around in short order. When Sir Andrew loses track of what's going on, he just repeats everything that Sir Toby says. Sir Toby has even convinced the knight that he has a chance of marrying Olivia.

Skill with a sword is another courtier's ability that Sir Andrew would like to have. As Maria says, he loves to start a quarrel. Since he can't fight, he has to talk or buy his way out of trouble. We see evidence of this when he offers "Cesario" his horse if the boy will agree not to fight him.

Sir Andrew is too much of a simpleton to be blamed for his actions. Most readers regard him with amused sympathy. He knows that others call him a fool. He even admits that he worries on occasion that he may be no smarter than anybody else! Still, he cannot or will not see himself as he is. At the end of the play, this upstart knight has been punished for his vanity by being beaten by Sebastian and rejected by Sir Toby. Shakespeare never tells us whether he learns anything from his ordeal. Do you think he would? Did he deserve his punishment?

Maria

Though she is Olivia's servant, Maria has most of her scenes with Sir Toby. She represents a balanced middle ground between Malvolio's insistence on decorum and Sir Toby's total disregard for manners.

We see Maria make several attempts to reform Sir Toby, or at least keep him out of trouble. She warns him that Olivia will not stand for much more of his drunkenness. Later, she tries to quiet Sir Toby, Sir Andrew, and Feste before they wake Malvolio.

Once Malvolio threatens her, however, Maria becomes the chief troublemaker. Malvolio has barely left the room before she has invented the plan to make a fool of him. Then she carries out her practical joke like a veteran prankster.

Maria is as clever with words as Sir Toby is. Look at Act I, Scene iii. She does not let Sir Toby confuse her with his word games. She makes sure he hears exactly what she has to say to him. Then, when Sir Andrew comes in, she puts him down so skillfully that at first he doesn't even realize that she's done it. No wonder Sir Toby admires her.

Shakespeare must approve of Maria's blend of manners and mischief. By the play's end she has been rewarded twice. She has gotten her revenge on Malvolio, and Sir Toby has married her. She has achieved exactly the change in class by marriage that Malvolio wanted for himself. Do you think she deserves her "reward"?

Feste

Feste is Olivia's "allowed fool," or clown. He entertains the other characters with songs, jokes, and puns. While he has access to all the various groups, he belongs to none. Therefore, he has a perspective that the others all lack. (For more about the role of the fool in Elizabethan society, see "The Author and His Times" section of this book.)

Under the guise of making jokes, Feste accurately evaluates the behavior of those around him. It's interesting to observe how the different characters react to him. Olivia knows what Feste is doing and appreciates his skill. She even lets him instruct her. Malvolio doesn't want to hear the truth about himself, so he is uncomfortable around Feste. Sir Andrew makes a big show of admiring the fool's skill, but he can't tell when Feste is just making up nonsense. Sir Toby and Maria both match wits with Feste, quip for quip. Although Orsino has no interest in anything Feste has to say, he values the fool's ability to sing melancholy songs. Can you see any advantage to having the fool be the one in the play who sees the truth?

Sebastian

Viola's brother Sebastian serves an important plot function. She looks just like him when she disguises herself as a man. Therefore, she is taken for him and he for her. That confusion serves to bring several plot strands together.

In his nature as well as his appearance, Sebastian is like Viola. Brother and sister care about each other deeply. At the beginning, neither can rejoice at being rescued from the sea, because each thinks the other is dead. Because of their love for each other, their reunion at the end of the play becomes more than just a resolution of the plot. It is a touching and magical moment.

Other Elements

SETTING

When Viola crawls out of the sea after the ship-wreck, the Sea Captain tells her they are in Illyria. Though there was an actual Illyria on the coast of the Adriatic, you need not bother looking on a map. Shakespeare made sure that his audience could learn all it needed to know about the settings of his plays from listening to the text.

Shakespeare's Illyria is a fairy-tale land populated with dukes, ladies, knights, and jesters. You never meet any "average" citizens. All the characters are either nobles or servants, plus a few seamen (or pirates, depending on whom you ask).

Illyria's coast allows Viola and Sebastian to be washed ashore. Since the story has elements of fantasy, that unusual method of arrival is appropriate.

When the sea washes Viola ashore in Illyria, it is as if she is newly born. She acquires a new name, a new sex, and enters into a whole new world of fantasy.

This is the world of the Twelfth Night, the twelfth day of the Christmas season, a traditional time for masquerades and revels. In the play, practically everyone wears a mask or is disguised. Not all the characters realize this, however! Some of them are deceived about themselves as well as about others. As you read the play, try to see how reality and appearance are being confused.

Illyria is also an idyllic kingdom, suitable for romance. The scenes take place in palaces and gardens, music fills the air, and almost everyone is in love.

THEMES

Here are some of the major themes in *Twelfth Night*. Notice how they interweave and affect each other, much as the different plot lines do.

1. SELF-DECEPTION

This theme could also be called "What we are versus what we think we are." Several of the characters cling to false ideas about themselves. Much of the humor and also the pathos and sadness in the play derive from this fact. For example, Sir Andrew thinks he is a courtly gentleman. Actually, he is a clumsy simpleton. When he tries to live up to his self-image, he behaves foolishly. Malvolio has convinced himself that he is superior to those around him. Orsino thinks he loves Olivia, when, in fact, he is in love with love. Examine the characters to determine whether they see themselves as they are or as they would like to be.

Even when the characters are deceived by others, they are really victims of self-deception. Maria's letter only confirms what Malvolio has been telling himself already. Sir Toby takes advantage of Sir Andrew by telling him what he wants to hear.

2. KINDS OF LOVE

Most of the characters are in love, but that word means something different to each one.

Romantic Love. Orsino's hopeless passion for Olivia is a perfect example of Romantic, or Courtly, Love. Obstacles are the essence of Romantic Love. The beloved must be unobtainable. The lover must remain chaste and pine for the woman he cannot have. Olivia actually helps Orsino by refusing his suit. She gives him an excuse to spend all day enjoying the pangs of unrequited love.

Romantic love is also sudden and inexplicable. So it is that Olivia falls in love with Cesario. There is no reason for it—it is just a sudden, blind passion.

Mature Love. Though Viola's love for Orsino has a romantic obstacle (her disguise as a boy), her feeling is genuine. In his romantic haze, Orsino worries only about himself and his own feelings. Viola's mature love unselfishly puts Orsino's feelings before her own. If Olivia is what he wants, Viola will try to win her for him.

Brotherly Love. Sebastian and Antonio share a deep feeling for each other, which they call love. This love is not sexual. Today we would probably call this feeling friendship. It is a feeling of trust and a concern for the other person's well-being born out of the difficult experiences they have shared. Sebastian also knows that Antonio risked death for his sake.

Familial Love. Viola and Sebastian's deep sadness when each thinks the other has drowned is evidence of their love for each other. They are the only surviving members of their family. At the end of the play, Viola is as happy about finding her brother alive as she is about marrying Orsino.

3. THE DANGER OF VANITY

Vanity is really yet another kind of love—*self* love. The play suggests that vanity frequently causes people to make fools of themselves. Malvolio, for example, loves nobody but himself. He wants to marry Olivia only to raise his social status. He loves himself so blindly that he never stops to question the content of Maria's letter. As you read *Twelfth*

Night, look for the ways the characters' self love gets them into trouble.

4. THE IMPORTANCE OF LAUGHTER

Laughter in this play has a healing effect. Revenge is achieved not by fighting (not by serious fighting, anyway), but by practical jokes. Nobody is really hurt. Even Sir Andrew and Sir Toby's "bloody coxcombs" aren't serious injuries. Pride and jealousy do not lead to bloodshed. They provoke laughter. When the laughter dies down in Act V, many of the characters' problems are resolved happily. Olivia and Orsino forget their mistakes and joyfully accept their appropriate mates. Pride and deception are forgiven. Malvolio helps clarify this theme by refusing to see the humor in the joke that was played on him. Since he cannot laugh at his punishment, as one critic points out, he is prevented from accepting his reward. In honor of Malvolio we could also call this theme "the danger of taking yourself too seriously."

5. APPEARANCE VS. REALITY

This is one of the major themes of literature, a serious theme even in a comedy like this. We know from real life that appearances are often deceiving. In this play, deception is everywhere. The young boy may really be a girl. Or he may be her brother. That severe Puritan may be a vain social-climber. A letter that promises your fortune may be assuring your destruction. That fearsome swordsman challenging you to a duel may actually be a cowardly dolt. Or that coward you attack may be a brave young man who will give you a beating! You will notice as you read that in practically every scene, something (or someone) is not what it appears to be.

Some of the characters seem to have a better grasp of reality than others, and the more obvious disguises are least intended as deceptions. Viola's clothing may disguise her sex, but not her honest and virtuous nature. The fool, Feste, is the one who keeps pointing out that words can be as misleading as physical appearances.

6. THE MADNESS OF LOVE

Driven by love, the characters lose control. Olivia embarks on what any objective viewer would have to call a humiliating pursuit of a boy who is many ranks below her in social status. Orsino lies about all day listening to music. These two are not ordinary fools. They act foolishly because love overrides their saner judgment.

STYLE

The characters in *Twelfth Night* speak the language of love—poetry. They seem less concerned with what they have to say than with how beautifully they express it. Even the characters who speak in prose try to choose the most beautiful image or the perfect metaphor. Orsino, of course, spends all day making up love rhymes. But even Olivia's maid Maria has the skill to forge a properly poetic love letter. Let's examine briefly how Shakespeare uses language in this play.

Rarely is a statement made in a simple, declarative sentence. Instead, the characters communicate mainly through the use of the poetic techniques of metaphor and simile. Technically, a metaphor is a comparison made without using "like" or "as." For example, Orsino says in Act I, Scene i, that after seeing Olivia he was turned into a hart (a deer). Of course he was not literally transformed into an animal. He uses the image of a hunted animal to describe how he feels. A simile uses imagery in the same way, except that the speaker does use "like" or "as." When Viola says her sister "sat like Patience on a monument," she's using a simile.

Orsino's excessively flowery speech lets you know that he is in love with love. Viola's poise is revealed in her precise choice of words while she is carrying off her disguise. The poetic beauty of her speech when she talks about love demonstrates the depth of her passion. You know that Andrew is a fool because he tries so hard to speak beautifully and fails so miserably.

As you read each scene, ask yourself two questions. First, how are the characters using imagery to communicate? Second, what are you learning about the characters from the way they speak?

ELIZABETHAN ENGLISH

The way we use language changes. Differences in pronunciation and word choice are apparent even between parents and their children. If language differences can appear in one generation, it is only to be expected that the English used by Shakespeare four hundred years ago will diverge markedly from the English that is used today. The following information on Shakespeare's language will help a modern reader to a fuller understanding of *Twelfth Night*.

Word Classes
Adjectives, nouns and verbs were less rigidly confined to particular classes in Shakespeare's day.

Adjectives could be used as adverbs, as when "loud" occurs where today we would require "loudly":

> I speak too loud
>
> *(III, iv, 4)*

Adjectives could be used as nouns. In lines 90–91 of the same scene, Malvolio tells Fabian:

> Go off, I discard you: let me enjoy my private

where "privacy" would be used today. Nouns often functioned as verbs. In Act IV, Scene ii, line 94 "property" is used to mean "confine":

> They have here propertied me; keep me in darkness

and verbs could be used as nouns as in:

> . . . Make no compare
> Between that love a woman can bear me,
> And that I owe Olivia
>
> *(II, iv, 102)*

where "compare" is equivalent to "comparison."

Word Meanings

The meanings of all words undergo change, a process that can be illustrated by the fact that "nice" used to mean "wanton" and "small" meant "slender." Many of the words in Shakespeare still exist today but their meanings have changed. The change may be small, as in the case of "cars" meaning "carriages/chariots" in:

> Though our silence be drawn from us with cars, yet peace
>
> *(II, v, 60)*

or more fundamental, so that "complexion" (*II*, *iv*, 26) meant "general appearance," "silly" (*II*, *iv*, 46) meant "innocent," "admire" (*III*, *iv*, 152) meant "be amazed by," and "perspective" (*V*, *i*, 209) meant "distorting glass."

Vocabulary Loss

Words not only change their meanings, but are frequently discarded from the language. In the past, "leman" meant "sweetheart" and "sooth" meant "truth." The following words used in *Twelfth Night* are no longer common in English but their meanings can usually be gauged from the contexts in which they occur.

coistrel *(I, iii, 40)* fellow of low repute
kickshawses *(I, iii, 113)* insignificant trifles (from **quelque (choses)**
barful *(I, iv, 41)* very difficult
gaskins *(I, v, 24)* trousers, stockings for men
botcher *(I, v, 52)* tailor
cantons *(I, v, 294)* songs
maugre *(II, i, 153)* despite, in spite of
testril *(II, iii, 34)* small coin
cozier *(II, iii, 91)* cobbler
champaign *(II, v, 160)* open countryside
point-device *(II, v, 163)* exactly, precisely
welkin *(III, i, 59)* sky, heavens
haggard *(III, i, 65)* wild hawk
wainropes *(III, ii, 57)* strong ropes used to tie oxen or horses to a cart
bawcock *(III, iv, 114)* handsome man, dandy
tuck *(III, iv, 226)* sword
yare *(III, iv, 226)* quick, ready
duello *(III, iv, 314)* duel

malapert *(IV, i, 43)* pert, rude
shent *(IV, ii, 108)* scolded
bawbling *(V, i, 52)* insignificant, of little value
scathful *(V, i, 54)* destructive
brabble *(V, i, 63)* fight, quarrel
perpend *(V, i, 298)* listen attentively, evaluate
geck *(V, i, 342)* fool, idiot

Verbs
Shakespearean verb forms differ from modern usage in three main ways:

1. Questions and negatives could be formed without using "do/did," as when the Duke asks Viola:

> Died thy sister of her love?
>
> *(II, iv, 120)*

where today we would say "Did your sister die of love?" or where Sir Andrew Aguecheek insists:

> . . . I know not
>
> *(II, iii, 4)*

where modern usage demands: "I do not know." Shakespeare had the option of using forms **a.** and **b.** where contemporary usage generally permits only the **a.** forms:

a.	b.
What are you saying?	What say you?
What did you say?	What said you?
I do not love you	I love you not
I did not love you	I loved you not.

2. A number of past participles and past tense forms are used which would be ungrammatical today. Among these are: "hid" for "hidden" in:

Wherefore are these things hid?

(I, iii, 122)

"spoke" for "spoken" in:

As it is spoke

(I, iv, 20)

"took" for "taken" in:

He might have took his answer long ago

(I, v, 267)

"writ" for "written" in:

'Twas well writ

(III, iv, 38)

"forgot" for "forgotten" in:

Hast thou forgot thyself?

(V, i, 139)

and "broke" for "broken" in:

He has broke my head across

(V, i, 173)

3. Archaic verb forms sometimes occur with 'thou' and with third person singular subjects:

Knowest thou this country?

(I, ii, 21)

Present mirth hath present laughter

(II, iii, 47)

He hath better bethought him

(III, iv, 302)

Pronouns
Shakespeare and his contemporaries had one extra pronoun, "thou," which could be used in address-

ing a person who was one's equal or social inferior.
"You" was obligatory if more than one person was
addressed:

> My masters, are you mad?
>
> *(II, iii, 87)*

but it could also be used to indicate respect, as
when Antonio and Sebastian address each other:

> *Antonio:* If you will not murder me for my
> love, let me be your servant.
> *Sebastian:* If you will not undo what you have
> done . . .
>
> *(II, i, 34ff)*

Frequently, a person in power used "thou" to a
child or a subordinate but was addressed as "you"
in return. Thus the Duke addresses Cesario:

> Thou knowest no less but all
>
> *(I, iv, 13)*

whereas all the Duke's servants address him as
"you":

> Will you go hunt, my lord?
>
> *(I, i, 16)*

If "thou" was used inappropriately, however, it
could cause grave offence. Sir Toby knows this
when he persuades Sir Andrew to use "thou" in
his challenge to Cesario:

> . . . taunt him with the licence of ink: if thou
> thou'st
> him some thrice, it shall not be amiss . . .
>
> *(III, ii, 42–3)*

One further pronominal reference warrants a comment: "he/she" and "it" were often interchange-
able:

> . . . 'tis a fair young man
>
> > (I, v, 102)

and:

> What kind of woman is it?
>
> > (II, iv, 26)

Prepositions

Prepositions were less standardized in Elizabethan English than they are today and so we find several uses in *Twelfth Night* which would have to be modified in contemporary speech. Among these are: 'of' for 'by' in:

> A lady, sir, though it was said she much resembled me,
> was yet of many accounted beautiful
>
> > (II, i, 24–5)

'on' for 'from' in:

> There's a testril of me too
>
> > (II, iii, 34)

'on' for 'at' in:

> Even now, sir, on a moderate pace
>
> > (II, ii, 2)

'on' for 'of' in:

> What should I think on it?
>
> > (II, v, 28)

and 'to' for 'with' in:

> No man hath any quarrel to me
>
> > (III, iv, 228)

Multiple Negation

Contemporary English requires only one negative per statement and regards such utterances as:

> I haven't none

as nonstandard. Shakespeare often used two or more negatives for emphasis, as when Antonio asks Sebastian:

> Will you stay no longer; nor will you not that
> I go with you?
>
> *(II, i, 1–2)*

or when Sir Andrew asserts:

> Nor I neither
>
> *(II, v, 186)*

POINT OF VIEW

In *Twelfth Night*, Shakespeare takes a common-sense look at some of the foolishness inherent in human nature. He exposes the ways in which we fall prey to pride, vanity, and self-deception. Then, with a broad and tolerant smile, he forgives those faults.

This comedy never denies that life is full of problems. It acknowledges the fact that people cause each other pain. But, as we talked about in the "Themes" section, the wages of sin are not death, but embarrassment. Characters are exposed in all their foolishness before they can do real harm to themselves or anybody else.

The one sin Shakespeare cannot forgive is Malvolio's. The steward wants to stamp out all good humor. He remains a killjoy to the end. Unable to laugh at his own foolishness, he rejects Olivia's offer to make amends. Yet Shakespeare still has Orsino send a messenger to "make peace" with Malvolio as the play ends.

FORM AND STRUCTURE

Several different plot lines weave their way through *Twelfth Night*. At first they develop separately. Then, the various threads of the plot get tangled up. Finally, all the conflicts are resolved in quick succession.

The story lines may be grouped into what could be called the Romantic Plot and the Low Comic Plot. The lovers—Orsino, Olivia and Viola—are the principal participants in the Romantic Plot. This story deals with the complications arising out of Orsino's fixation on Olivia, and Viola's disguise. The Low Comic Plot involves the servants—Maria, Malvolio, Fabian—and the drunken knights—Sir Toby and Sir Andrew. The main action of this plot deals with the practical joke played on Malvolio. A second practical joke played on Sir Andrew draws the Romantic and the Low Comic plots together.

The play is shaped by the way these two plots are developed through the five-act structure.

Act I introduces the Romantic Plot. Its conflicts can be summed up like this: Orsino loves Olivia, who loves Viola, who loves Orsino. Thus, we have a comic version of the classic triangle made possible by the fact that Viola is disguised as a boy. Most of the characters involved in the Low Comic Plot are also introduced in Act I.

As **Act II** starts, we learn that Viola's brother Sebastian is on his way to Illyria. Then, Malvolio offends Maria and the others. The practical joke is planned. By the end of the act, Malvolio has been "set up." Meanwhile, the situation with Viola, Olivia, and Orsino gets more complicated.

In **Act III,** the practical joke pays off—Malvolio makes a fool of himself. Viola becomes entangled with the Low Comic characters. A case of mistaken identity draws Sebastian into the action too.

Act IV sets up the resolution. Sebastian and Olivia are thrown together. A promise of marriage is made. Malvolio's punishment continues.

In **Act V,** the conflicts are resolved when all the main characters are paired off with their proper mates. The comedy ends happily in marriage.

SOURCES

Most of Shakespeare's plots were borrowed from popular stories or actual histories. *Twelfth Night* was no exception. Plays about identical twins who are mistaken for one another had been popular since the time of the ancient Greeks. Shakespeare used the device himself in *The Comedy of Errors,* based on the *Menaechmi* by the Roman playwright Plautus. In that play, Shakespeare's first, the comic confusion is caused by twin boys. But the male/female variation was not original with Shakespeare. When John Manningham saw *Twelfth Night* on February 2, 1602, he noted in his diary the similarity between Shakespeare's play and an Italian comedy by Nicolo Secchi called *Gl'Ingannati*. That play also used disguised twins to further comic confusions among lovers. Most scholars believe that the romantic lovers' plot was based on a story by Barnabe Rich called

"Of Apolonius and Silla." However, the story of how the arrogant Malvolio gets his comeuppance was, as far as we know, created by Shakespeare.

THE GLOBE THEATRE

One of the most famous theaters of all time is the Globe Theatre. It was one of several Shakespeare worked in during his career and many of the greatest plays of English literature were performed there. Built in 1599 for £600 just across the River Thames from London, it burned down in 1613 when a spark from one of the cannons in a battle scene in *Henry VIII* set fire to the thatched roof. The theater was quickly rebuilt and survived until 1644. No one knows exactly what the Globe looked like but some scholarly detective work has given us a pretty good idea. The Folger Shakespeare Library in Washington, D.C., has a full scale re-creation of the Globe.

When it was built, the Globe was the latest thing in theater design. It was a three story octagon, with covered galleries surrounding an open yard some 50 feet across. Three sides of the octagon were devoted to the stage and backstage areas. The main stage was a raised platform that jutted into the center of the yard or pit. Behind the stage was the tiring house—the backstage area where the actors dressed and waited for their cues. It was flanked by two doors and contained an inner stage with a curtain used when the script called for a scene to be discovered. (Some scholars think the inner stage was actually a tent or pavillion that could be moved about the stage.) Above the inner

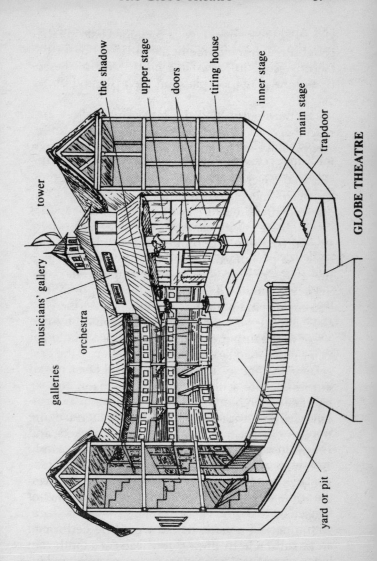

the shadow

upper stage

doors

tiring house

inner stage

main stage

trapdoor

tower

musicians' gallery

orchestra

galleries

yard or pit

GLOBE THEATRE

stage was the upper stage, a curtained balcony that could serve as the battlements in *Hamlet* or for the balcony scene in *Romeo and Juliet*. Most of the action of the play took place on the main and upper stages.

The third story held the musicians' gallery and machinery for sound effects and pyrotechnics. Above all was a turret from which a flag was flown to announce, "Performance today." A roof (the shadow) covered much of the stage and not only protected the players from sudden showers but also contained machinery needed for some special effects. More machinery was under the stage, where several trap doors permitted the sudden appearance in a play of ghosts and allowed actors to leap into rivers or graves, as the script required.

For a penny (a day's wages for an apprentice), you could stand with the "groundlings" in the yard to watch the play; another penny would buy you a seat in the upper galleries, and a third would get you a cushioned seat in the lower gallery—the best seats in the house. The audience would be a mixed crowd—sedate scholars, gallant courtiers, and respectable merchants and their families in the galleries; rowdy apprentices and young men looking for excitement in the yard; and pickpockets and prostitutes taking advantage of the crowds to ply their trades. And crowds there would be—the Globe could probably hold 2000 to 3000 people, and even an ordinary performance would attract a crowd of 1200.

The play you came to see would be performed in broad daylight during the warmer months. In colder weather, Shakespeare's troupe appeared indoors at Court or in one of London's private theaters. There was no scenery as we know it but there are indications that the Elizabethans used simple set pieces such as trees, bowers, or battle tents to indicate location. Any props needed were readied in the tiring house by the book keeper (we'd call him the stage manager) and carried on and off by actors. If time or location were important, the characters usually said something about it. Trumpet flourishes told the audience an important character was about to enter, rather like a modern spotlight, and a scene ended when all the characters left the stage. (Bodies of dead characters were carried off stage.) Little attention was paid to historical accuracy in plays such as *Julius Caesar* or *Macbeth* and actors wore contemporary clothing. One major difference from the modern theater was that all female parts were played by young boys; Elizabethan custom did not permit women to act.

If the scenery was minimal, the performance made up for it in costumes and spectacle. English actors were famous throughout Europe for their skill as dancers and performances ended with a dance (or jig). Blood, in the form of animal blood or red paint, was lavished about in the tragedies; ghosts made sudden appearances amidst swirling fog; thunder was simulated by rolling a cannon ball along the wooden floor of the turret or by rattling a metal sheet. The costumes were gorgeous—and expensive! One "robe of estate" alone cost £19, a year's wages for a skilled workman of the time. But the costumes were a large part of the spectacle that the audience came to see, and they had to look impressive in broad daylight, with the audience right up close.

You've learned some of the conventions of the

Globe Theatre, a theater much simpler than many
of ours but nevertheless offering Shakespeare a wide
range of possibilities for staging his plays. Now
let's see how specific aspects of *Twelfth Night* might
have been presented at the Globe.

Shakespeare wrote his plays for a repertory company, and often you can tell something about the
actors from the way the characters in the plays are
described. For example, at the time Shakespeare
wrote *Twelfth Night*, there must have been a small,
dark boy in the company. Several of the plays
Shakespeare wrote around this time have female
characters (played by boys) who are described as
particularly short and dark, like Maria. Actors in
Shakespeare's day specialized in certain kinds of
parts. The comic actor Thomas Pope created the
role of Sir Toby Belch and was also the first Fal-
staff. At this time, Robert Armin had joined the
company as the "clown," replacing the hilarious
but unreliable Will Kempe. He was apparently a
good all-round actor as well as a comedian, because Shakespeare began to use the clown as a
character in plays such as *Twelfth Night*, and not
merely as a bit of comic relief.

Twelfth Night also provides a good illustration of
the Elizabethan love of music. The play is filled
with songs, dance, and instrumental music that
must have kept the musicians in the Globe's third-
story gallery busy. Plays like this made the playhouse popular with foreign visitors, who could enjoy the costumes and the music, and the slapstick
comedy of scenes like the duel between Sir Andrew and Viola, even when they couldn't understand English.

The Play

ACT I

In Act I, you meet most of the principal characters. Orsino, the Duke of Illyria, loves the countess Olivia. She will not have him, and he can think of nothing but her. Viola, a nobly born young lady from another country, is cast on the Illyrian shores by a shipwreck. For safety's sake, she disguises herself as a boy and becomes Orsino's servant. The situation becomes complicated when Orsino sends his new servant as a messenger to Olivia. Believing Viola to be a boy, Olivia falls in love with "him." You also meet the comic collection of servants and relatives who make up the rest of Olivia's household.

ACT I, SCENE I

Lines 1–24

Orsino, Duke of Illyria, listens to his musicians play a melancholy tune. When he speaks, we learn that he craves melancholy music—music with a "dying fall" (cadence)—as a starving man craves food. His opening line is a famous one: "If music be the food of love, play on."

Orsino is completely captivated by thoughts of love. It would not be an exaggeration to say he seems to worship love. Love is like the sea, he says; that is, it can encompass anything. Compared to love, he claims, anything else is worthless.

One of Orsino's servants tries to distract him by

suggesting they go hunting, but the duke quickly changes the subject back to love by saying that he is hunted by his own desires. Not until he has finished his lengthy description of his own emotions does he mention the name of his beloved—Olivia.

Lines 25–43

A messenger returns from Olivia's house with the news that he was not allowed to see her. Her maid gave him this message: Olivia intends to keep to herself and mourn her brother's death for seven years.

Her attitude is just as exaggerated as Orsino's, but still he finds hope in this message. If she shows so much dedication to a brother, he reasons, just think how faithful she will be to a husband! This new idea seems to inspire Orsino to change his locale. Off he goes to "sweet beds of flowers."

The Orsino we meet in this scene is not in love with Olivia, or any real person. He is in love with love. Notice that his elaborate speech in praise of love comes before any mention of the lady. Notice also that he makes no attempt to see Olivia himself. He sends a messenger instead. Her inaccessibility gives him the opportunity to enjoy his unrequited love.

NOTE: On excess   The imagery in Orsino's speeches reveals his character. He asks for "excess" in line two, and everything he does is excessive. Because he is in love with Olivia, he must spend all day consumed with "love-thoughts" (*line 43*). He does not merely have desires. He has desires which chase him "like fell and cruel hounds" (*line* 23). Though Orsino is a grown man, he sounds like a love-sick adolescent.

Excess runs through the entire play, and is an important idea. Olivia's decision to mourn her brother for seven years is excessive. As new characters are introduced, try to determine which ones behave in an excessive manner and which ones attempt to cope sensibly with excessive behavior in others.

ACT I, SCENE II

On the seacoast of Illyria, a young girl, a sea captain, and some sailors have just emerged from the ocean. Their ship was sunk in a storm. They were lucky to avoid drowning.

The girl is more unhappy than relieved, however, because her brother was not as lucky as the others. When she is told they are in Illyria, she says her brother is in "Elysium," that is, heaven. The Captain offers her hope: he says he saw her brother tie himself to a piece of the ship's mast, so he may have survived.

Feeling a little better about her brother's situation, the girl, Viola, turns her attention to her own predicament. The Captain knows Illyria. He tells her that it is ruled by a noble duke named Orsino. According to the latest gossip, the Captain says, Orsino is in love with Olivia, "a virtuous maid" whose father and brother have both died within the year.

Viola is in a difficult position. She is a young woman in a strange land with no family to protect her. Therefore, she does not want to reveal who she is right away. Her first idea is to temporarily become a servant of Olivia's. The Captain, however, tells her that Olivia will not see anybody.

In desperation, Viola invents a plan. With the Captain's help, she will disguise herself as a boy and present herself to Orsino. (She says she will present herself as a eunuch, a castrated youth. This part of the plan is never mentioned again after this scene, however.)

You learn several important facts about Viola in this scene. First, she is a young woman of noble birth. The Captain treats her with great respect, and she is able to reward his kindness with gold. Second, she cares deeply about her brother. Her own escape from death is meaningless to her until she learns that her brother may have survived also. Finally, she is sensible and resourceful. She is smart enough not to reveal her true identity until she knows more about the people around her. Look how quickly she comes up with the idea of disguising herself as a boy.

Shakespeare uses the imagery of Viola's speech to suggest that she is suited to Orsino. Remember the music in the first scene? Look at what Viola says: "I can sing,/And speak to him in many sorts of music."

NOTE: By having Viola pretend to be a boy, Shakespeare sets up the comic confusion that will follow. When *Twelfth Night* was performed in the Elizabethan theater, there was another wrinkle in the comedy. Acting was not considered a respectable profession for a woman. All the female parts were played by young boys. So, in this play, a young boy played a young girl who disguised herself as a young boy!

ACT I, SCENE III

Lines 1–43
The action now moves to Olivia's house, but you do not yet meet the lady herself. Instead, you are introduced to one of her servants, Maria, and one of her "poor relations," Sir Toby Belch. Sir Toby complains that his niece Olivia's mourning is taking all the fun out of the house. Maria counters that Sir Toby is having *too much* fun—drinking and partying every night—and that he had better reform because Olivia will not take much more.

Maria dislikes Sir Toby's companion, Sir Andrew Aguecheek. She calls him "a very fool and a prodigal." Sir Andrew, according to her, is a quarreler, a coward and a drunk. Sir Toby disagrees, claiming that his friend is cultured, wealthy and well-educated.

NOTE: Observe how evenly matched Sir Toby and Maria are. They treat each other like equals. Her criticism is direct and forceful, definitely not servile! His deflection of her assaults is skillful. For example, Maria tells Sir Toby: "you must confine yourself within the modest limits of order" (*lines 8–9*). Sir Toby pretends to misunderstand her, replying "I'll confine myself no finer than I am" (*line 10*), playing on the fact that the word "confine" also meant "clothe." When Maria says that Sir Andrew is "drunk nightly in your company," Sir Toby replies that they are "drinking healths [that is, toasts] to my niece" (*lines 36–38*).

Lines 44–78

The debate about Sir Andrew is interrupted by the arrival of the man himself. It quickly becomes obvious that Maria's description of him is correct. He attempts to flirt with Maria by showing how clever he is, but he fails miserably. Sir Toby advises him to "accost" Maria (in other words, "go get her"). Sir Andrew thinks "Accost" is her name. Once that confusion is cleared up, Sir Andrew presents Maria with additional opportunities to make a fool of him. She takes advantage of every one. For example:

> *Andrew:* Fair lady, do you think you have
> fools in hand?
> *Maria:* Sir, I have not you by th' hand.
> (*I, iii, 64–65*)

By the time Maria leaves, Andrew has been thoroughly deflated.

Lines 79–136

Sir Andrew and Sir Toby are left alone. We see why Sir Toby likes the young knight—Sir Andrew is his puppet. He can be persuaded to believe anything the older man says. Sir Toby knows that Sir Andrew is a fool, but a useful fool. The one true thing Sir Toby told Maria was that Sir Andrew is rich.

First, Sir Andrew announces that he is going home. Sir Toby brought him here to woo Olivia, and he has had no success. In fact, he has just found out that Orsino himself wants her. Sir Toby replies that she does not want Orsino. He says that Sir Andrew has hope. With that, the knight decides to stay another month!

Then Sir Andrew, who is probably still smarting from Maria's insults, begins to praise his own virtues. Sir Toby distracts him from any further complaints by getting him to demonstrate his dancing ability. As you read the scene, picture how comically clumsy Sir Andrew must be and with what a smirk Sir Toby must praise his puppet's skill.

It is appropriate that, at the end of their first scene together, Sir Toby has Sir Andrew literally dancing to his commands. Sir Andrew figuratively dances to Sir Toby's commands throughout the play.

NOTE: The double plot   *Twelfth Night* has two main plots—the Romantic and the Low Comic. The Romantic plot concerns the high born lovers— Orsino, Viola, Olivia, and, later, Viola's brother Sebastian. The Low Comic plot revolves around the characters we've just met. Fabian and Malvolio will also play important parts in this plot.

If you examine the way this scene is laid out on the page, you will notice that it is in prose, unlike the previous two scenes. They were written in blank verse—unrhymed iambic pentameter (lines with ten syllables, every second syllable accented). Shakespeare commonly wrote most of the speeches for his noble upper-class characters in verse, while the lower-class and comic characters spoke in prose. In this play, the nobles speak mostly in verse, though they have prose passages, also. The low comic characters all speak only in prose.

ACT I, SCENE IV

Viola, now calling herself Cesario, has entered Orsino's service. The scene begins with one of the other servants commenting on how remarkable it is that "Cesario" should have become so well-liked in only three days. Viola asks whether the duke is inconstant (fickle) in his affections. Having met Orsino in the opening scene, we can appreciate the ironic humor in the servant's answer "No, believe me."

Orsino enters. He confirms the fact that "Cesario" is his favorite by sending the other servants away so he can talk to the "boy" alone. You observe how close the duke and Cesario have become when Orsino says "I have unclasped/To thee the book even of my secret soul" (*lines 13–14*). He means, of course, that he has told Cesario about Olivia and his love for her. Now, he wants Cesario to be his messenger to his lady.

Viola reasonably points out that Olivia refuses to see anybody. Orsino's answer fits his tendency to excess: "Be clamorous and leap all civil bounds/Rather than make unprofited return" (*lines 22–23*). He seems confident that Cesario will succeed where others have failed.

Orsino also believes that, due to Cesario's youth and his almost feminine (!) beauty, the boy will be a fitting messenger of love. Orsino promises to reward Cesario if he is successful.

Before Viola/Cesario leaves, she pauses for an

aside.[Asides are a theatrical convention in which the character speaks directly to the audience. The other characters do not hear an aside.] Viola tells us that she will have a hard time wooing Olivia on Orsino's behalf. Her problem is that she has fallen in love with him herself!

NOTE: Observe how skillfully Shakespeare draws you into his plot. The idea of a girl disguised as a boy being in love with her master but having to woo another lady for him sounds hard to believe. But by working his way into the situation step by step (from Orsino's helpless love, to Olivia's denial, to Viola's shipwreck and need for disguise), Shakespeare makes the situation seem logical, almost inevitable.

One reason why it is hard to take Orsino's love for Olivia too seriously is that at the end of the play he turns to Viola so easily. But consider the way he has been treating "Cesario" in this scene. Orsino finds the boy a perfect person to talk to, someone he can really feel comfortable with. Should you be surprised when he offers Viola his love?

ACT I, SCENE V

Lines 1–30

Back in Olivia's house, Maria is scolding Olivia's Clown, Feste, for being absent when the lady was looking for him. The two trade quips, with Maria trying to make the Clown realize he's in trouble, and the Clown expressing his confidence that his foolery will save him from punishment.

NOTE: In this play the terms "Clown" and "Fool" have the same meaning. A "fool" was another name for a jester. He was employed to amuse a noble or wealthy person. Fools in Shakespeare's plays were generally wise fools. Feste may be the wisest of them all. Under the guise of foolery, he tells the truth about people and situations. If you have ever known a person able to cut a braggart down to size or make a good point with a well-chosen joke, then you know the function of a Shakespearean fool.

Lines 31–100

Olivia enters with her steward Malvolio. As Maria predicted, Olivia is angry. Her first words are "Take the fool away."

Feste's method of dealing with Olivia's anger shows us a lot about his methods. He responds quickly in a seemingly absurd fashion. Turning to the guards, he says "Do you not hear, fellows? Take away the lady." This bit of silliness does not amuse Olivia. Brushing aside her criticisms, Feste keeps insisting that *she* is actually the fool. Olivia gives in enough to allow the fool a few moments to prove his claim. To do so, he questions her:

> *Clown:* Good madonna, why mournest thou?
> *Olivia:* Good fool, for my brother's death.
> *Clown:* I think his soul is in hell, madonna.
> *Olivia:* I know his soul is in heaven, fool.
> *Clown:* The more fool, madonna, to mourn for
> your brother's soul being in heaven.
> Take away the fool, gentlemen.
>
> *(I, v, 67–73)*

Feste's tactic works. Olivia is no longer angry.

What do you learn about Feste from this exchange? You see his ability to show people their own foolishness. Notice how familiar he is in the way he speaks to Olivia. You will see that Feste can move freely and comfortably from one social level to another.

Olivia appreciates the fool's ability. He both amuses her and gives her comfort about her brother. His jest can also be seen as a gentle hint that Olivia's announced seven years of mourning are excessive and unnecessary.

Malvolio is not amused. He insults the fool, asserting that he recently saw Feste "put down" (defeated in jesting) by "an ordinary fool that has no more brain than a stone." Malvolio brags that he is too smart to be amused by a fool.

Olivia sees her steward for what he is: "O, you are sick of self-love, Malvolio, and taste with a distempered appetite." She knows that Malvolio is jealous of anybody who is considered clever. He is so pompous he cannot stand even gentle ribbing.

Lines 101–169

Maria brings word that a new messenger from Orsino waits at the gate. Sir Toby Belch, she says, is dealing with him. Olivia also knows her uncle for what he is: "Fetch him off, I pray you. He speaks nothing but madman." She orders Malvolio to get rid of the messenger.

Sir Toby reels in, already drunk though it is only morning. Olivia asks "how have you come so early by this lethargy?" meaning his drunkenness. He responds "Lechery? I defy lechery." Is he purposely avoiding her question, or is he too drunk

to know the difference? You have to decide. In
either case, he soon staggers off.

NOTE: Some readers view Sir Toby and Sir Andrew as representatives of knighthood in decline.
Compared to the Middle Ages, the Renaissance
was a relatively peaceful time. Knights were no
longer called upon to quell rebellions or venture
off on Crusades in the Holy Land. The two knights
in this play have nothing to do but eat, drink, and
sleep. Though Sir Toby is intelligent and resourceful, even brave, he performs no useful function in
Olivia's household.

Olivia reveals a compassionate nature in her response to Sir Toby. He annoys her, and she may
wish he were not living in her house, but she worries about his welfare nonetheless. She sends the
fool to look after him.

A moment later, Malvolio returns. He hasn't been
able to get rid of the messenger. Whatever Malvolio has said, the man has had an answer for it.
You know that the messenger is Viola and that
she's following Orsino's orders by refusing to take
"no" for an answer.

Olivia inquires what this messenger is like. As
fits his nature, Malvolio is reluctant to give any
information at all. When Olivia insists, he cannot
say anything nice ("He is very well-favored")
without adding something nasty ("He speaks very
shrewishly"). Olivia's curiosity wins out over her

reticence. She covers her face with a veil, calls for Maria to join her, and tells Malvolio to let the messenger in.

Lines 170–221

Viola enters as Cesario. Olivia intends to have this messenger deliver his speech and leave, but Viola is too clever. She insists on being told whether the person she addresses is actually Olivia. After all, she says, she took a lot of time and trouble to memorize her speech. She would hate to waste it. Olivia reveals her identity.

Viola's next task is to talk with the lady privately. She banters engagingly with Olivia and Maria. Finally, her request for a private audience is poetic enough to be successful: "What I am, and what I would, are as secret as maidenhead: to your ears, divinity; to any other's, profanation." Maria leaves.

Lines 222–294

Now Olivia believes she is alone with a young man. She continues to insist that she cannot love Orsino, but she is strangely fascinated by this messenger.

Viola has said that her words would be divinity to Olivia's ears, so Olivia begins by questioning her like a preacher giving a sermon (from the question in line 222, "What is your text?" to her conclusion in line 230 "It is heresy!").

Changing the subject, Viola asks Olivia to remove her veil. Olivia grants the request. In the discussion that follows, Viola is honest to the point of being rude. She begins by saying Olivia's face is "Excellently done, if God did all." After listening to Olivia, she concludes that the lady is "too proud" but concedes she is beautiful.

Olivia admits in turn that Cesario's master is a fine man. She lists all his virtues (possibly to prevent Cesario from doing it). But she firmly states that she still cannot love him.

Viola counters that Olivia's refusal makes no sense. Robbed of any other argument, she tells the lady what she (Cesario) would do in Orsino's situation. Her statement takes the form of a hauntingly beautiful verse about the loneliness of rejected love.

Olivia is clearly moved. She asks Cesario about his family. (In that time, the social status of your family determined your social status.) Olivia then sends Cesario back to Orsino to say she cannot love him. He is also never to send a messenger again, *unless* it is Cesario. Viola refuses Olivia's offer of payment and leaves.

NOTE: You learn a great deal about Viola while she's in disguise. Though she plays the role of a young boy, she displays her own wit, spirit, and passion. She knows how to be humble and charming, as when she says she doesn't want to waste her speech because she took such pains to learn it. She can also be direct, as when she accuses Olivia of being too proud. Finally, you feel the depth of Viola's passion when she describes what she would do in Orsino's place. The passionate intensity of the speech may partly be due to the fact that Viola cannot speak of love to Orsino.

Lines 295–318
Left alone, Olivia is shocked to discover that she has fallen in love with Cesario! Taking a ring off her finger, she calls in Malvolio. She tells him that Cesario left a ring with her as a gift from Orsino. She orders him to follow the messenger and return the ring. The truth, of course, is that she is sending the ring as a gift to Cesario.

Olivia's speech after Malvolio leaves points up a major theme in the play. She says "I do I know not what" and "Ourselves we do not owe (own)." Many of the characters in this play do not understand themselves. For example, Orsino thinks he is in love with Olivia, but he is really in love with love. Malvolio thinks he is virtuous, whereas in reality he is a self-righteous hypocrite. They deceive themselves. Look for other examples.

NOTE: Olivia's character   Until this scene, you had heard about Olivia but never met her. Once she appears, you learn a lot about her very quickly. She is beautiful, witty, rather impetuous. Shakespeare lets you see several sides of her personality. She begins the scene angry, is kidded into a good humor, plays with Cesario, and by the end of the scene you even see her in love. Read the scene again to determine how each of these points about her character is revealed.

Another point about Olivia: some readers believe that her intention to mourn her brother for seven years is merely a ruse, a way of attracting attention. They point to the fact that she falls in love so quickly as proof. Do you think she knows what she's doing, or that, as she says, her behavior confuses even her?

ACT II

At the beginning of Act Two, you meet Viola's twin brother, Sebastian, who is on his way to Illyria. Meanwhile, Orsino continues to use Viola as his messenger to Olivia. Olivia's steward Malvolio reprimands Toby, Andrew, Feste, and Maria when he catches them carousing in the middle of the night. Maria, who was only there trying to quiet the others, invents a plan to take revenge on Malvolio. She forges a letter from Olivia and leaves it where Malvolio will find it. Malvolio falls for the trick and believes that the letter is evidence that Olivia loves him.

ACT II, SCENE I

This short scene between Viola's brother Sebastian and Antonio, the man who rescued him from the shipwreck, tells you several important things. First, you learn that Sebastian is still alive. You also learn that he and his sister look very much alike. In a production of *Twelfth Night*, Viola and Sebastian would wear identical costumes. This similarity will become important later in the play.

Sebastian cares as deeply for his sister as she does for him. He assumes she is drowned, and when he talks about her he has a hard time to keep from crying.

Another important thing you learn is that Sebastian is heading for Illyria. He wants to go alone and refuses to explain his reasons for going. You can guess that he may hold some desperate hope that his sister may have made it to the shore in that country. He may not want to admit that he still clings to such a slim hope.

Sebastian's friend and rescuer, Antonio, cannot follow him there. He says he has "many enemies in Orsino's court." At the last minute, however, he decides to follow his friend despite the danger.

NOTE: The actions of Sebastian and Antonio constitute a subplot. Shakespeare wants you to notice who these two are and to remember the nature of their relationship. That's why this scene appears where it does. Note that the next scene (II, ii) completes the action started in the scene before this. By inserting this exchange between Sebastian and Antonio in the middle, Shakespeare calls attention to it.

ACT II, SCENE II

Malvolio catches up with Viola on the street outside Olivia's house. With a sneer, he follows his lady's orders and "returns" the ring. Viola finds the situation confusing. She plays along, refusing to take the ring back (since she never gave it to her in the first place). Malvolio rudely drops the ring to the ground and walks off.

Lines 17–41
Viola's confusion does not last long. She quickly figures out that Olivia has sent her a love gift. Her

situation is going from bad to worse! Not only is she in love with a man who thinks she is a boy, but now the woman *he* loves is in love with Viola.

She blurts out "Disguise, I see thou art a wickedness/Wherein the pregnant enemy does much." Viola means her own disguise as a man, but the statement has a wider thematic meaning in the play. Viola's disguise causes problems, but the false appearances of others (see discussion of Act I, Scene v) get them into just as much trouble.

Her head swimming, Viola takes a moment to sum up the situation. She must admit that it is a mess and that she has no idea what the solution will be.

NOTE: Although Malvolio has played a relatively minor role so far, he is being set up as a character who is arrogant, rude and conceited. Shakespeare is preparing you to enjoy the trick that will soon be played on Malvolio.

Shakespeare has now presented all the elements of his Romantic plot: Orsino loves Olivia, who cannot love him; Viola loves Orsino, who thinks she is a boy; Olivia loves Viola, who she thinks is Cesario; and Viola's double (Sebastian) is on his way to Illyria.

ACT II, SCENE III

Now the Low Comic plot begins in earnest. At Olivia's house, Sir Toby and Sir Andrew are up late drinking. Sir Andrew may have just suggested that he would like to go to bed, because Sir Toby is busy explaining why being up late is the same thing as being up early. Sir Andrew is too slow to follow this reasoning, but he will go along with whatever his friend says.

Lines 15–86
Feste soon joins the party. Notice how Sir Andrew responds to the clown. He envies Feste's ability to sing and dance. And the fool knows he has a good customer in Sir Andrew. Whatever nonsense the fool spouts, Sir Andrew finds hilarious.

NOTE: There are two fools in this scene—Feste and Sir Andrew. As a "wise" fool, Feste is essentially an entertainer. He amuses you with his wit. A "natural" fool like Andrew is funny in spite of himself. He amuses you because he is witless. Shakespeare's other wise fools include Touchstone in *As You Like It* and the Fool in *King Lear*. Other examples of natural fools are William in *As You Like It* and Dogberry in *Much Ado About Nothing*.

At Sir Toby and Sir Andrew's request, the fool sings two songs. The first could be considered a summation of the Romantic plot: "O mistress mine, where are you roaming?" Orsino, Olivia and Viola are each seeking the right love mate. The second song has more to do with the Low Comic characters. "Present mirth hath present laughter;/What's to come is still unsure," sings Feste. Today you might say "Have fun now; who knows what will happen tomorrow?" That seems to be Sir Toby's philosophy.

After the fool's solo, all three join in a "catch," or "round." The noise has awakened Maria, and she comes in to warn them that they had better be quiet before they wake up Malvolio. They are too lost in merrymaking to pay any attention. A few moments later, Malvolio himself appears.

Lines 87–126

Nobody looks his best at four in the morning, and you can picture how ridiculous Malvolio must appear, standing in his nightgown. Looking bleary-eyed but stern, he shouts "My masters, are you mad? or what are you?" Sir Toby, Sir Andrew and Feste dissolve into helpless laughter. As Malvolio scolds them, they laugh, sing and make fun of him. A man like Malvolio, who is "sick of self-love," does not like being mocked, especially in the middle of the night. Sir Toby goads him further by directly attacking Malvolio's sense of self importance: "Art any more than a steward? Dost thou think, because thou art virtuous, there shall be no more cakes and ale?" Sir Toby is reminding Malvolio that, as a knight, his social position is well above that of a steward. Malvolio behaves as though he *were* Olivia and had her authority, which he does not. What's more, Sir Toby bellows, just because you choose to be so pompous and insufferable, don't expect others to follow suit.

Mortally offended, Malvolio threatens to tell Olivia about the episode. He also includes Maria in his wrath, because she was there and failed to help him.

Lines 127–191

His final threat was a mistake. As soon as Malvolio leaves, Maria invents a plot to get even with him.

(Sir Andrew comes up with a confused plot to challenge Malvolio to a duel and then make a fool of him by not showing up, but you already know not to take Sir Andrew seriously.)

Maria's plot works like this: she will prepare a letter that appears to have been written by Olivia. The letter will make Malvolio believe that Olivia is in love with him. Maria knows the truth about Malvolio—that despite the fact he behaves like a Puritan, he really deceives himself into thinking that other people find him witty, charming and attractive. Therefore, he will fall for the trick and make a fool of himself in front of Olivia.

NOTE: Maria's personality encompasses two extremes. She performs her duties with decorum and even takes it upon herself to try to reform Toby. She also has a mischievous sense of humor. This scene demonstrates both sides of her nature. She enters for the same reason as Malvolio—to impose order. Once angered, however, she becomes the chief prankster. There is no real malice in her joke. She only wants to teach Malvolio a lesson.

After Maria leaves, the carousing resumes. You learn that Sir Toby is aware that Maria loves him. You are also informed that Sir Andrew has loaned him a great deal of money.

NOTE: You are continually reminded how witty Sir Toby is, even when he's drunk. In line 177, he calls Maria "Penthesilea." He refers to the queen of the Amazons, a race of gigantic warrior women. The comment works in two ways. On one hand, there is ironic humor in the fact that Maria is physically quite small. On the other hand, she's a formidable warrior in the battle against Malvolio.

ACT II, SCENE IV

Lines 1–49

Back in Orsino's palace, you find that nothing has changed. Orsino is still calling for music and talking about nothing but love. He asks for a melancholy song he heard the night before. His servants go to find Feste, the clown, to sing it. (Though Feste is Olivia's fool, you never know where he will be found.) While they search, Orsino orders the musicians to play the tune.

Cesario (Viola) comments that the tune "gives a very echo to the seat/Where Love is throned." Orsino is surprised that the boy knows so much of love, and asks about the one Cesario loves. Though Viola says she loves a person of the same age and temperament as Orsino, he fails to realize the truth.

The irony in this scene is that Viola actually feels the same way Orsino thinks he feels. She wants him just as desperately as he thinks he wants Olivia. She patiently listens as he lectures her about love, a subject she already knows about from firsthand experience.

Lines 50–98

Feste enters and sings the song Orsino has asked for. It is indeed melancholy, telling the story of a young man who died for the love of a woman.

NOTE: This song linking love and death serves two functions. To Orsino, dying for love represents the ultimate expression of his romantic indulgence. For Viola, the meaning is more profound. She understands romantic longing, because she loves Orsino but cannot have him. She also realizes that love, youth, and beauty are like fair flowers that "die, even when they to perfection grow." This awareness of the inevitability of aging, death, and decay enriches the play and deepens its portrayal of the human condition. It serves as a melancholy counterpoint to the broadly comic scenes.

After hearing the song, Orsino tells Viola to take another message of love to Olivia.

Lines 99–140
Viola now has several reasons for not wanting to go. She desires Orsino herself, she knows his suit to Olivia is hopeless and, finally, she knows that Olivia loves Cesario. She tries to convince Orsino to give up. In doing so, she almost tells him the truth about her love for him.

First, she asks him to imagine that a woman loved him as he loves Olivia. If he could not love her, that woman would have to accept his refusal, Viola tells him. Orsino counters by saying that no woman could love a man as powerfully as he loves Olivia.

Now, Viola knows he is wrong. She tells him a carefully worded story about her "father's daughter" who loved a man. She even goes so far as to add "As it might be perhaps, were I a woman/I should your lordship." This "daughter" never revealed that she was in love. Instead, she pined away with grief, the same thing Orsino is doing.

Still seeking to prove that women cannot love as deeply as men, Orsino asks, "But died your sister of her love, my boy?" Orsino overlooks the fact that, despite all his sighing and moaning, he is still alive and well. "I am all the daughters of my father's house/And all the brothers too, and yet I know not" is Viola's answer. Speaking so directly about her love for Orsino and being reminded that her brother is probably dead is too much for Viola. If she continues talking, she will cry. Bowing to Orsino's wishes, she goes to speak with Olivia.

NOTE: This scene contrasts Viola's deep and real love for Orsino with his imagined love for Olivia. Viola's love leads her to unselfishly put Orsino's desires before her own. She talks with him about his feelings and acts as his messenger. Her pain is intensified by the fact that she cannot even speak of her love, except indirectly, as she does here. Orsino is only in love with love. At this point, he really cares for nobody besides himself.

ACT II, SCENE V

Lines 1–21
In Olivia's garden, Sir Toby and Sir Andrew wait for Maria. They are joined by Fabian, another of Olivia's servants who hates Malvolio. Malvolio seems to have told Olivia that Fabian was involved in bear baiting. To be fair, bear baiting was a cruel sport, though very popular. The point is not Fa-

bian's taste in games, however. You are reminded that Malvolio is a "snitch" and a killjoy.

Maria runs in, just ahead of Malvolio. She tells the other three to hide. Malvolio, she says, has been "practicing behavior to his own shadow this half hour." In other words, he has been admiring himself, so she knows he's ripe for the joke about to be played. She places the phony letter on the ground where he will see it, and she leaves.

Lines 22–175
As he enters, Malvolio is talking to himself. Thinking he is alone, he speaks his true thoughts. The man you see is a far cry from the Puritan he pretends to be when other people are around. He is daydreaming about a time when Olivia will marry him and make her her equal. He takes the fact she treats him with respect as a sign that she loves him. (He *says* she treats him better than she treats anybody else, but we have to suspect he is deceiving himself.) Caught up in his fantasy, Malvolio imagines the other members of the household bowing to him. He sees himself ordering Toby to give up drinking.

NOTE: Malvolio talks about marrying Olivia, but he never mentions *loving* her. As far as you can tell from this soliloquy, he is motivated solely by ambition. His self love seems to have rendered him incapable of loving anybody else. That could explain why the others dislike him so. On the surface, they want revenge on him for spoiling the fun. On a deeper level, they may hate and fear him because he represents cold-hearted ambition untempered by concern for his fellow man.

Remember that Toby, Andrew and Fabian are watching and listening. They make comments to each other as they listen and only hold themselves back from attacking Malvolio in order not to ruin the joke. Fabian's comment is especially accurate: "Look how imagination blows him." Malvolio's imagination gives him an "inflated" idea of who he is.

Then Malvolio spots the letter. He picks it up and begins to read. Malvolio is quickly convinced that the letter is Olivia's—the handwriting looks like hers, the choice of words sounds like hers and the letter is closed with her seal. So far, the plan is working. The three men spying on him can hardly contain themselves.

Can you imagine how Malvolio must feel? While daydreaming that Olivia loves him, he finds a letter addressed "To the unknown beloved"! Opening the envelope, he finds a poem that begins "Jove knows I love—/But who?" A few lines later it reads "I may command where I adore." Putting two and two together, Malvolio comes up with the answer he wants—he himself is the object of his lady's affections. Of course Olivia may command anybody in her household. Malvolio is only reaching the conclusion he wants to reach.

Look how completely Malvolio has now been taken in. The next line of the poem gives him a little trouble, but he is determined to make it work out. "M.O.A.I. doth sway my life." Fabian calls it a "fustian riddle;" in other words, nonsense. Malvolio simply observes that "M" is his initial and the other letters are all in his name somewhere, so she must mean him. Maria was right—he is *very* ripe for this joke.

The poem is followed by some prose. This part of the letter appears to be Olivia's instructions to Malvolio about what he should do to be worthy of her love. Maria, of course, chose all the things Olivia would hate most. First, Malvolio is told "Be opposite with a kinsman, surly with servants. Let thy tongue tang arguments of state; put thyself into the trick of singularity." That's like telling a butler or a waiter to argue with his patrons instead of serving them.

Next, he is instructed how to dress. He is to wear yellow stockings and to cross his garters both above and below the knee. (Little does he know that Olivia hates yellow stockings and crossed garters.)

The letter ends with an appeal to Malvolio's ambition:

> Go to, thou art made, if thou desir'st to be so.
> If not, let me see thee a steward still, the fellow
> of servants, and not worthy to touch Fortune's
> fingers.

This last challenge was hardly necessary. Malvolio cannot wait to follow the instructions in the letter.

He finds a postscript that tells him that, if he wants to show his love for Olivia, he should smile constantly. You can imagine that Malvolio, who always frowns, looks even worse trying to smile. Also, Olivia is in mourning. Smiling would be out of place, even insulting. He has been completely fooled, however. As he leaves he promises to do everything the letter asks of him.

NOTE: Malvolio jumps at the letter's suggestions so eagerly that he almost appears to be a willing accomplice in his own deception. Though the letter is a phony, it works by appealing to Malvolio's true nature. Maria's assessment of his character was correct. His puritanical behavior is an act. He assumes a solemn countenance merely to intimidate others. Therefore, this practical joke serves a positive purpose—the exposure of hypocrisy.

Lines 176–203:
Sir Toby, Sir Andrew and Fabian roll with laughter at their joke. Sir Toby swears he could marry Maria for having thought of it. Maria comes in, and Sir Toby begins to praise her. Sir Andrew echos everything the older man says. Maria reviews the things that the letter asks Malvolio to do and the reasons that Olivia will hate them. Then, they all go to watch Malvolio make a fool of himself.

NOTE: To appreciate the humor of this scene you must use your imagination while reading it. Picture Malvolio completely entranced by the letter while the others laugh and whisper to each other. Occasionally, Malvolio might hear a noise and turn around, causing the others to dive for cover. One classic joke in productions of *Twelfth Night* is for Malvolio to turn when the others have no time to hide. In that case, they each assume a pose like a statue in the garden. Malvolio is too self-absorbed to notice anything unusual!

ACT III

Maria's joke works. By following the instructions in the letter, Malvolio makes a fool of himself in front of Olivia. Viola's brother Sebastian and his friend Antonio arrive in Illyria. They separate, because Antonio will be arrested if he is seen there. Another practical joke begins when Andrew sees how lovingly Olivia receives "Cesario." Toby and Fabian convince the knight to challenge the boy to a duel. Before they can fight, however, Antonio mistakes Viola for her brother and intervenes. Antonio is recognized by Orsino's officers and arrested.

ACT III, SCENE I

Lines 1–70
Viola (as Cesario) arrives at Olivia's house. She finds Feste outside playing his drum. As the two talk, we learn more about both of them.

It becomes clear that the fool's art is to take advantage of the fact that a word can mean many things or nothing at all. Every question Viola asks is twisted by Feste into a different meaning.

> *Viola:* Dost thou live by thy tabor (drum)?
> *Clown:* No, sir, I live by the church.
> *Viola:* Art thou a churchman?
> *Clown:* No such matter, sir. I do live at my
>   house, and my house doth stand by
>   the church.
>
> *(III, i, 1–7)*

"Live by" can mean "make a living with," as Viola intends, or "live near," the meaning Feste answers.

Viola quickly sees what the fool is doing. She agrees that words are dangerous, because clever people can make them mean anything they like. Viola's awareness of that fact helps her survive in this tricky situation. Notice how precisely she chooses her words in her scenes with Orsino and Olivia.

Feste even points out the different meanings of the word "fool." Viola asks "Art not thou the Lady Olivia's fool?" Feste will not accept the title. Olivia's husband, when she takes one, will be her fool, he says. Feste is her "corrupter of words."

Afraid that she will become the butt of his jokes, Viola gives him a coin and asks him to leave. Feste's cleverness gets him another coin. Then he goes into the house to announce Cesario's arrival.

After he leaves, Viola's comments show a real appreciation for the fool's art. She realizes that his jests are not just random comments. The fool's skill, she says, demands careful observation of the people he jests about. To be a good fool "is a practice/ As full of labor as a wise man's art."

NOTE: Shakespeare himself can be seen as a "fool," in a way. *Twelfth Night* seems to be a comedy about foolish people—love-sick nobles, drunken knights, girls who dress as boys, pompous servants, and so forth. Clearly, Shakespeare wanted to make his audience laugh, and he succeeded. But at the same time he is commenting on the nature of love, the meaning of maturity, and the dangers of vanity and self-deception.

Lines 71–96
While Viola is waiting in the garden, Sir Toby and Sir Andrew enter. Sir Andrew addresses Viola in French. He is just showing off and assumes that

the boy will not understand him. Sir Andrew is impressed when Viola answers him in French. Having used up the little French he knows, he is barely able to get out an appropriate answer in English. Sir Toby steps in and asks Viola to enter the house. Just as she is about to do so, Olivia and Maria come out.

Viola's formal way of greeting Olivia impresses Sir Andrew even more than her speaking French. He is about to try to top her when Olivia orders everyone out except herself and the messenger.

Lines 97–173

Olivia now believes she is alone with the boy she loves. She asks for his hand, and she asks his name. Viola complies formally, saying that she is doing her duty and that she is Olivia's servant. Olivia wants to be more direct. She corrects "Cesario," saying that he is Orsino's servant. "Your servant's servant is your servant, madam," replies Viola. Olivia responds sharply, declaring that Cesario should never mention Orsino again.

Becoming even more direct, Olivia asks Cesario to "undertake another suit" than Orsino's (i.e., to declare his own love for Olivia). That would delight her as much as "music from the spheres." Olivia goes on to apologize for her boldness in sending the ring to Cesario. She admits her love for the boy and asks him to tell her how he feels about her.

What can Viola say? She cannot love Olivia, nor can she explain why. There is no way in the world for Olivia to get what she wants from "Cesario." Viola says what she feels: "I pity you." Olivia finds hope in that statement, pointing out that pity is "a degree to love." Viola explains that there is *no* hope. She reminds the lady that people often pity their enemies.

Olivia seems to give up. She says she will not spend any more time being unhappy over Cesario. Admitting that she envies the woman who will one day marry Cesario, she sends him on his way.

Viola knows how much it would mean to Orsino to have some message from Olivia. Before she goes, she asks if the lady has no word for her master. In that moment of delay, Olivia loses her self-control. She blurts out "Stay/I prithee tell me what thou thinkst of me." The exchange that follows is a masterpiece of double meaning:

> *Viola:* That you do think you are not what you are.
> *Olivia:* If I think so, I think the same of you.
> *Viola:* Then think you right. I am not what I am.
> *Olivia:* I would you were as I would have you be.
> *Viola:* Would it be better, madam, than I am? I wish it might; for now I am your fool.
>
> (III, i, 148–153)

Viola's frustration builds as she answers as honestly as she can but is not understood. Olivia's passion mounts, because she cannot understand why this proud youth is rejecting her. Finally, Olivia makes an all-out declaration of love. She swears by everything she holds dear that in spite of Cesario's proud refusal to love her, she cannot help loving him.

Cesario takes an equally strong oath that no woman will ever be mistress of his heart. As the "boy" turns to go, Olivia uses the one weapon she has left. Knowing that this messenger is genuinely concerned for his master, she says that if he will come back another time, he may win her heart for Orsino.

Take a moment to look at Viola's line "You do think you are not what you are," because it sums up a major theme of the play. How many of the other characters could you say the same thing about? Malvolio thinks he is something he's not, and so do Orsino and Sir Andrew. See if you think that description fits any of the others.

ACT III, SCENE II

Sir Andrew Aguecheek spied on Olivia and Cesario during the last scene. He is furious, because Olivia, who is barely even polite to him, fawned all over Cesario. As this scene begins, Sir Andrew is angrily swearing to leave Olivia's house right away. Sir Toby and Fabian are trying to talk him out of it.

Lines 1–65
After Sir Andrew explains why he is so upset, Fabian asks whether Olivia knew he was watching. Sir Andrew vows that she did (although from reading the scene we have to assume that he only imagines she saw him). Fabian turns the situation upside down by insisting that what Sir Andrew saw was actually proof that Olivia loves him.

Olivia, he asserts, was only trying to make Sir Andrew jealous by treating Cesario so well. He claims that Sir Andrew missed a golden opportunity to prove his love for Olivia. He should have rushed in and used his wit to put Cesario down completely. (Does that sound to you like something Sir Andrew could have managed?) Having missed his cue, he will have to make up for it "by some laudable attempt either of valor or policy." In other words, he must either challenge Cesario to a duel (valor) or outsmart him (policy).

Sir Andrew takes the bait. He hates "policy" (can we blame him?), so it has to be "valor." Sir Toby coaches him in how to compose a properly fearsome challenge. Sir Andrew goes off to write it.

After he leaves, Fabian and Sir Toby laugh about the joke they are playing. Fabian calls Sir Andrew a "dear manikin," but Sir Toby explains that he is more than a toy—he is also a ready source of money. Sir Toby promises to deliver Sir Andrew's challenge to Cesario, but he's sure the two will never fight. "For Andrew," says Sir Toby, "if he were opened, and you find so much blood in his liver as will clog the foot of a flea, I'll eat the rest of the anatomy."

NOTE: Why is Sir Andrew so lacking in the skills a knight should possess? Since he comes from a wealthy family, you would expect him to have received the proper training. His ineptness could be due to his stupidity. There is another possible explanation. In Elizabethan England, a rich but untitled person could raise his social status by purchasing a title. Perhaps the wealthy Andrew is Shakespeare's parody of a cloddish commoner who has bought his noble rank but cannot so easily acquire the courtly graces to go with it.

Lines 66–83
Maria dashes in, helpless with laughter. She has
news of their other prank. Malvolio has followed
every one of the instructions in the letter. He is
walking around in yellow stockings and crossed
garters and smiling like an idiot. All three run off
to see him.

NOTE: The pace of the Low Comic plot is quick-
ening. Just when a new jest is added, the first joke
begins to pay off. As you read, take notice of the
rhythm Shakespeare establishes as he cuts back
and forth between his various plots. You may find
it confusing. Remember that, in production, the
distinctive appearance of each character would help
you to keep track of what is going on. Forming
clear mental pictures of the thin, pale Sir Andrew,
the fat Sir Toby, the prissy Malvolio, etc., might
help you as you read.

ACT III, SCENE III

Viola's brother Sebastian and his friend Antonio
arrive in Illyria. Antonio has just caught up with
Sebastian. He explains that he followed along partly
out of concern for Sebastian, who doesn't know
his way around. But he says his main reason for
coming was his love for his friend.

NOTE: Shakespeare is introducing another kind
of love into the play. The other characters are in-

volved in Romantic love. What Antonio and Sebastian feel for each other is friendship or brotherly love. Their shared experiences have given them true trust and affection for each other. This fact will sharpen Antonio's reactions when the confusion begins in the next scene.

Sebastian is touched by Antonio's devotion to him. He proposes a tour of the town. Antonio admits he must not be seen in Illyria. He once took part in a sea battle against Orsino's navy. If caught, he faces serious consequences.

The two plan to separate for an hour. Antonio will go to a tavern called the Elephant while Sebastian looks around the town. Antonio wants Sebastian to have his purse, in case he wants to buy anything.

NOTE: The Sebastian/Antonio plot will eventually blend with the Romantic plot. You have been told that Sebastian and Viola are now both in Illyria and that they look exactly alike. What you do not yet know is how Shakespeare will use their physical similarity.

ACT III, SCENE IV

Lines 1–17

A feeling of anticipation hangs over this scene. In her garden, Olivia waits for Cesario. She sent a servant to bring him back before he could reach Orsino's palace. How will she win the boy over, she wonders? Since rejection has made her sad, she asks for Malvolio. His seriousness will suit her mood.

Maria anticipates what will happen when the "new" Malvolio comes in. Of course, she must not betray her excitement. Feigning innocence, she tells Olivia that Malvolio is behaving strangely and smiling constantly. Olivia asks to see him.

NOTE: Speaking of Malvolio, Olivia says "I am as mad as he,/If sad and merry madness equal be." *Twelfth Night* can be seen as a wonderful demonstration of both kinds of "madness." Orsino and Olivia are mad with lovesick sadness. Sir Toby and Sir Andrew seem mad in their drunken merrymaking. Malvolio's madness ranges from his exaggerated solemnity in the beginning to the "merry madness" produced by the letter.

Lines 18–67
Dressed in bright yellow stockings and smiling like an idiot, Malvolio almost dances in. He is certain that Olivia loves him. When she asks "Wilt thou to bed, Malvolio?" meaning "You seem to need some rest," he replies "To bed? Ay, sweetheart; and I'll come to thee."

His true pride reveals itself in the way he answers Maria:

> *Maria:* How do you do, Malvolio?
> *Malvolio:* At your request? Yes, nightingales
>   answer daws!
>
>   (III, iv, 37–39)

Though they are both servants and equals, Mal-

volio behaves as if he were far superior. True, he
does what the letter told him, but he has secretly
felt superior all along.

Though Olivia is shocked, her compassion shows
itself again. Malvolio has gone crazy. She is wor-
ried about him. When a servant arrives to announce that he has—with *great* difficulty—brought
Cesario back, Olivia sends Maria to fetch Toby.
She wants her uncle to take special care of Malvolio. (Remember how she sent Feste to look after
Toby?)

NOTE: Reason for Malvolio's behavior   You have
to ask why Malvolio, who always behaves in such
a proper fashion around others, can be so easily
gulled into acting foolish. Why do you think he
accepts the letter without reservation or suspicion?
Could it be because he *wants* the letter to be true?
Or does his ambition to be great override any cau-
tion? Certainly he refuses to see that Olivia treats
him like a madman. Is he so vain it never occurs
to him the letter could be a fake? After all, Maria
claims in Act II, Scene iii that Malvolio believes that
"all that look on him love him." In that case, he
might assume that Olivia is playing with him. One
thing is clear—vanity has made Malvolio blind to
reality.

Lines 68–146
Left alone, Malvolio marvels at how well things
are working out. He assumes that Sir Toby has
been sent for so that Malvolio can be rude to a
kinsman, as the letter advised.

He does just that when Sir Toby, Maria and Fabian enter. They pretend to be very concerned for him, but he rudely says "Go off; I discard you."

Sir Toby, Maria, and Fabian are now in exactly the position they've longed for—they can mock Malvolio to their hearts' content. Hovering about him, they tell him he is possessed by the devil. They treat everything he says as the raving of a madman. Finally, Malvolio has had enough. "I am not of your element," he tells them. That is, "I am better than you." And he leaves.

The three conspirators are delighted. Their joke is working better than they had dared hope. Sir Toby proposes that they use the excuse of Malvolio's madness to have him locked away in a dark cell.

NOTE: Sir Toby wants to extract as much revenge from the scheme as he can, but he isn't heartless. The joke is "for our pleasure and his penance," says Sir Toby. He sees the prank as a way for Malvolio to atone for his sins. Eventually they will "have mercy on him."

Lines 147–202

Before they can pursue their prey, Sir Andrew struts in. He has just written his challenge to Cesario and is very proud of it. When Sir Toby reads the letter aloud, it quickly becomes clear that all Sir Andrew has accomplished is to prove what a fool he is. The wording of the challenge ranges from confusing to laughable.

Sir Toby and Fabian praise Sir Andrew's writing.

Maria says that Cesario is with Olivia even as they
speak. Sir Toby sends Sir Andrew to lie in wait for
Cesario outside the garden. He advises the knight
to draw his sword and swear loudly as soon as he
sees Cesario.

Once Sir Andrew has gone, Sir Toby reveals that
he has no intention of delivering the letter. Cesario, he says, would realize that it came from an
idiot. He will, however, make Sir Andrew's challenge for him verbally. In doing so, he will convince Cesario that Sir Andrew is a fearsome opponent.

Lines 203–410
Just then, Olivia and Cesario enter the garden. Sir
Toby, Fabian, and Maria sneak off to make up a
challenge.

Olivia tells Cesario that she fears she has been
too open with him. Her love for him is so strong
that she simply cannot be cautious, she says.

Viola replies by once again pleading Orsino's
cause. "With the same 'havior that your passion
bears/Goes on my master's grief." Olivia gives a
picture of herself to Cesario and asks him to come
again tomorrow. Her parting line confirms how
smitten she is: "A fiend like thee might bear my
soul to hell." She would not only give up all her
worldly goods for the boy, but give her soul to the
devil!

NOTE: This brief scene underlines the ways that
Orsino and Olivia are similar. They are both af-
flicted with the "sad madness," as Viola points
out. They also share a liking for excess. Is Olivia
really prepared to go to hell for the love of this

messenger boy, or is she indulging herself in the same way Orsino is when he talks about dying for love?

As soon as Olivia leaves, Sir Toby and Fabian dash in to tell Cesario that a valiant and deadly knight challenges him to a duel. Sir Toby says he doesn't know what Cesario did to offend him, but the knight is very angry. He is determined to have blood. Sir Toby describes Sir Andrew as a master swordsman who has killed three men.

Viola is terrified. First, she tries to go back to the house, but Sir Toby will not let her. Then, since she is sure she has not done anything to offend anybody, she asks Sir Toby to find out why this knight is so angry. He agrees to ask, and goes off, leaving Fabian to make sure "Cesario" does not run away.

Fabian adds to Sir Toby's portrait of Sir Andrew: "He is indeed, sir, the most skillful, bloody, and fatal opposite [opponent] that you could possibly have found in any part of Illyria." He promises to try to make peace, if he can, and asks Viola to follow him.

Meanwhile, Sir Toby tells the same lies to Sir Andrew about Cesario. Sir Toby claims he fought with the boy and barely escaped with his life. Hearing this, Sir Andrew wants to drop the whole matter. Sir Toby warns him that Cesario is so angry that he's determined to fight. Fearing for his life, Sir Andrew offers to give Cesario his horse if he will forgive the offense. Sir Toby says he will convey the message.

Fabian arrives with Viola. She and Sir Andrew

are equally terrified. In order to coax them into fighting, Sir Toby tells each one that the other promises not to hurt him.

NOTE: A sequence like this practical joke on Sir Andrew and Viola serves to remind you that Shakespeare had an actor's understanding of stagecraft. The comedy of this passage is mainly physical. It provides wonderful acting opportunities for the players. Try to imagine how a good comic actor would portray Sir Andrew's swift shift from swaggering challenger to fearful coward, or what tone of voice the actor playing Sir Toby would use to frighten his two victims.

The two trembling adversaries reluctantly inch towards each other. Just as they are about to clash, Viola cries "I do assure you 'tis against my will." At that moment, Antonio walks in. He thinks he sees his friend Sebastian being forced to engage in a sword fight. Antonio leaps to his friend's rescue.

Sir Toby steps in to confront Antonio, possibly because he knows that Sir Andrew could never defend himself against a real swordsman. But before they can begin fighting, two officers arrive to arrest Antonio. As he feared, he has been recognized as an enemy of Orsino's. Antonio tries to bluff his way out of his predicament, but he quickly sees that it's hopeless.

Regretfully, he asks "Sebastian" (who is actually Cesario, who is really Viola!) to return his purse. Viola appreciates Antonio's coming to her aid as he did, but she has no idea what he means when he asks for his purse.

Antonio is stunned. He can't understand why this man he has loved as a brother should betray him now in his hour of need. Just before the officers drag him off, Antonio rebukes his friend. In doing so, he says the name Sebastian.

Now it is Viola's turn to be stunned. She could see that this man believed he knew her. What's more, he called her Sebastian. Could she, dressed as a man, have been mistaken for her brother? She is hopeful, but cautious. She still has no proof that her brother lives.

NOTE: Contrast Viola's reaction to being called by her brother's name with Malvolio's response to finding Maria's letter. Each is being told what he or she wants to believe. Viola wisely realizes that things are not always what they appear to be. Malvolio lacks that wisdom. Therefore, Viola can keep her balance in a difficult situation, while Malvolio contributes to his own downfall.

After Viola leaves, Sir Toby and Fabian pick up the pieces of their joke. They say that Cesario has proved himself a coward by failing his friend. If the man is a coward, Sir Andrew will fight him. Off he goes after Cesario, followed closely by Sir Toby and Fabian.

NOTE: In this long scene, all the plot strands become entangled. Viola has been drawn into the action of the Low Comic characters. Antonio, who was previously only involved with Sebastian, is now mixed into the other plots. You know that each of these characters will draw others in. Whatever affects Viola will affect both Olivia and Orsino. Sebastian will have to find out what happened to his friend Antonio.

The motifs of confusion and deception rapidly "snowball" to great comic effect. Shakespeare has laid the groundwork in earlier scenes. By this point, every character is either being deceived or is deceiving somebody else. Viola does both—she deceives Olivia and is deceived by Toby and Fabian. Every action in the entire scene is based on some kind of mistake.

ACT IV

The confusion continues when Sebastian is mistaken for his sister Viola. After being threatened by Sir Andrew and Sir Toby, Sebastian is taken by Olivia into her house. Then Feste helps Sir Toby and Maria to further punish Malvolio, who has been locked up as a madman. When you next see Sebastian, he is trying to figure out if he has gone mad. Olivia has asked him to marry her. Though Sebastian is stunned and confused, he is also delighted and so he accepts.

ACT IV, SCENE I

Lines 1–23

Now that Viola has been mistaken for Sebastian, it's time for Sebastian to be taken for her. As this scene begins, Feste believes he is talking with Cesario. In fact, he's talking to Sebastian. Each thinks the other is crazy. Feste tells "Cesario" that Olivia wants to see him. Sebastian says that Feste is talking nonsense. In his frustration, Feste declares "Nothing that is so is so."

NOTE: It's no mistake that Feste did not appear in the previous scene. The action of that scene deepens the confusion. The characters cling to their misconceptions. Feste provides perspective. He seems to play with, rather than become involved with, the other characters. Notice that as soon as the Fool reappears, he delivers a piece of "nonsense" that clarifies the situation: "Nothing that is so is so."

Lines 24–70

Sir Andrew runs up and makes the same mistake as Feste. Thinking he's caught up with the cowardly boy, he walks right up to Sebastian and hits him. Sebastian now thinks everybody has gone crazy. He hits Sir Andrew back. Once again, Sir Toby comes to Sir Andrew's defense. Feste runs off to tell Olivia what is happening.

Just as Sir Toby and Sebastian draw their swords, Olivia enters. She can't believe her eyes. Sir Toby is trying to hurt her beloved Cesario! Olivia gives her uncle a good scolding and orders him and his friends to leave.

Then she turns to comfort the man she believes is Cesario. Lovingly, she apologizes for her uncle. She practically begs "Cesario" to come into her house.

Sebastian concludes that he either has gone mad
or is dreaming. But if it *is* a dream, he prefers to
stay asleep. He enjoys the attention he's getting
from this beautiful woman. Olivia is delighted that
"Cesario" finally responds to her affection. The
scene ends with two surprised but happy people.

NOTE: Shakespeare wrings the last ounce of humor out of the disguises by piling mistake upon
mistake. Sir Andrew is always wrong about his
opponent. When he thinks Cesario is a great
swordsman, the boy is actually a frightened girl.
When he decides Cesario is a coward, Sebastian
has taken his sister's place, so Sir Andrew gets a
beating.

ACT IV, SCENE II

Lines 1–74
Shakespeare now turns his attention back to Malvolio and yet another disguise. Maria has locked
up the steward in a dark cell. Her plan calls for
Feste to disguise himself as a priest—Sir Topas.
While Toby and Maria watch, "Sir Topas" visits
the prisoner.

Feste uses his skill at twisting the meanings of
words to torment Malvolio:

> Malvolio: Sir Topas, Sir Topas, good Sir
>   Topas, go to my lady.
>   Clown: Out, hyperbolical fiend! How vexest
>   thou this man! Talkest thou nothing
>   but of ladies?
>
> *(IV, ii, 24–27)*

When Malvolio complains about being locked in

a darkened cell, Feste insists that the cell has huge windows and is full of light.

Malvolio wants to prove his sanity by answering a question about philosophy. Feste asks him such a question, then twists Malvolio's answer into further proof that he's mad.

Sir Toby and Maria enjoy the joke, but Sir Toby says it's time to call a halt. The fight with Cesario has gotten him into trouble with Olivia. He tells Feste that he wants to let Malvolio out before things get worse. Sir Toby and Maria leave.

Lines 75–135

Feste displays even more skill when he returns to Malvolio without the disguise. Taking advantage of the fact that Malvolio cannot see him, he plays both himself *and* Sir Topas.

Malvolio asks the fool to bring him a pen, ink, some paper and a candle. He wants to write a letter to Olivia. Pleading with the fool, Malvolio says he is being tormented by "ministers . . . asses."

Just then, thanks to Feste's acting ability, "Sir Topas" appears. He reprimands Malvolio and tells the fool not to speak with him.

When Malvolio thinks the priest has left, he offers the fool money to take the letter for him. Feste decides to help Malvolio. Singing a song, he goes off to get the pen and paper.

Notice how responsive Feste is to money. His need or desire to be paid helps to remind us that he's human. Though he often seems removed from the foibles of ordinary people, he has his own failings too.

NOTE: Is Malvolio's punishment too harsh for his crime? Some readers consider him an almost tragic figure. All he really wants is to better himself. That's a common human desire. It was especially popular in the nineteenth century to take a sympathetic view of Malvolio. Later readers have disputed that view as overly sentimental. They hold that he's a cold-hearted, mean-spirited hypocrite who gets what he deserves, much to everyone's delight. It's not unusual for Shakespeare's characters to be reinterpreted in different eras. For example, in Shakespeare's theater, Shylock in *The Merchant of Venice* was played broadly with heavy makeup as a figure of fun. Today, Shylock is considered a profoundly human and tragic character.

ACT IV, SCENE III

In Olivia's garden, Sebastian tries to figure out what is happening to him. To get his bearings, he looks around. Air is still air, he says. The sun looks like it always has. But why has Antonio vanished? And why should a noble and beautiful lady want to marry him after knowing him for only a few seconds? He doesn't think he's crazy, and the lady seems sane, but *something* strange is happening.

Olivia enters with a priest in tow. She wants "Cesario" to swear before the priest that he will marry her. Sebastian has apparently fallen in love with Olivia as quickly as she fell in love with "Cesario." He follows her off to make the promise. This scene offers the first hint of the happy ending to come. None of the confusions have been resolved. The situation will get worse before it gets better. But Olivia now has a suitable mate, and he wants to marry her.

NOTE: Though you may not realize it, you are taking an active role in all the scenes of mistaken identity. The actors cannot look exactly alike, of course. In real life no male and female, even twins, could be mistaken for one another. Shakespeare makes it very clear that you *should* believe it, though. For the sake of enjoying the fun of the play, you do. That process is sometimes called "willing suspension of disbelief."

ACT V

Orsino, accompanied by Viola, visits Olivia. In one long scene, all of the confusions are resolved. After being reunited with her brother, Viola reveals her true identity. She and Orsino will wed, as will Olivia and Sebastian. You learn that Toby has already married Maria. Malvolio is released from prison and the joke played on him is explained. Though Olivia tries to appease his anger, Malvolio is too proud to forgive those who humiliated him. He stalks off. The others leave to prepare for the double wedding. Feste ends the play with a song.

ACT V, SCENE I

Lines 1–102
In front of Olivia's house, Fabian tries to get Malvolio's letter away from Feste. They are interrupted by Orsino, Viola, and Orsino's other servants. Orsino finally has come to see Olivia himself.

The duke knows Feste. As the two banter, Feste sneaks in another bit of wisdom under the guise

of nonsense. He says that he is better off because
of his enemies and worse because of his friends.
Orsino says the fool must mean the opposite. Look
at Feste's explanation:

> Marry, sir, they [my friends] praise me and make
> an ass of me. Now my foes tell me plainly I am
> an ass; so that by my foes, sir, I profit in the
> knowledge of myself, and by my friends I am
> abused.
>
> (V, i, 17–20)

Impressed by the fool's logic, Orsino gives him
a coin. Feste begs another. Then he goes in to tell
Olivia that she has a visitor.

NOTE: Feste points up a major theme in the play—
the danger of vanity. Malvolio and Sir Andrew,
for example, both suffer because they believe they
are better than they really are. You could say the
same of Orsino. His indulgence in suffering the
pangs of unrequited love is an act of vanity. He
would profit if somebody would tell him he's acting like an ass.

At that moment, the officers drag Antonio in.
Viola testifies that he is the man who helped her.
Orsino knows him as an enemy. He calls Antonio
a pirate.

NOTE: Some readers object to the fact that you
never get to know much about the nature of Antonio's offense against Orsino or his supposed reasons for opposing the duke. Shakespeare only tells

you enough to justify his use of Antonio in the plot. It is interesting that, in a play that makes so many implausible actions seem believable, Shakespeare lets Antonio remain a bit of a loose end.

Antonio denies that he ever was a pirate, though he *was* Orsino's enemy. He bitterly accuses "that most ungrateful boy there," who he thinks is Sebastian, of betraying him. He claims to have taken care of the boy for three months. Orsino says the man is mad. The boy has been *his* servant for three months.

Lines 103–184
Olivia's entrance takes Orsino's attention away from Antonio. The lady doesn't want to hear Orsino's vows of love. That's hardly surprising. She has refused to hear them for months now. What *is* unusual to Orsino is that Olivia seems much more interested in Cesario than she is in him. She even interrupts the master to ask the servant to speak.

Orsino begins to realize what has happened—that Olivia loves Cesario. He reminds Olivia of a legendary Egyptian who tried to kill a woman when he could not have her. But Orsino will not do that. Instead, he will "sacrifice the lamb that I do love [Cesario]" to spite Olivia. He starts to leave. Viola follows, vowing that she would gladly die for the love of Orsino.

Olivia is shocked. Cesario is going back on his word. Calling him "husband," she summons the priest who confirms that Olivia and Cesario exchanged vows only two hours before.

Never has Orsino been so abused! Instead of

wooing his lady for him, Cesario married her himself. Orsino cannot believe that such a young boy can be so evil. What will he be like when he grows up, Orsino wonders?

Lines 185–220
Suddenly, Sir Andrew runs on, crying out for a surgeon. Both he and Sir Toby have had their heads split open by Cesario, he cries. Imagine Sir Andrew's surprise when he looks up and sees Cesario staring at him. Sir Toby comes in next, drunk and bleeding. Feste has to hold him up.

Sir Toby has apparently been pushed to the breaking point, because he becomes honest. When Sir Andrew offers to help him, he harshly replies "Will you help—an ass-head and a coxcomb and a knave—a thin-faced knave, a gull?" Olivia orders that Sir Toby be looked after. Feste, Sir Toby, Sir Andrew, and Fabian all leave.

NOTE: The foolish knight   You have now seen the last of Sir Toby and Sir Andrew. However, you will hear more of Sir Toby. Sir Andrew can be got rid of, because he only served to add humor. There is no need to resolve the question of whether he will be successful in wooing Olivia. He never stood a chance.

Sir Toby's last line to Sir Andrew is cruel but honest. Following Feste's reasoning from the beginning of the scene, Sir Toby does Sir Andrew a favor. He finally tells him plainly he is an ass. We have no scenes to indicate whether Sir Andrew profits from this honesty. Whatever he does, though, it could not be worse than what he did while Sir Toby falsely flattered him.

Lines 221–348
As they go, the man who really beat them—Sebastian—walks in. He apologizes to Olivia for hurting her uncle. He had no choice, he explains. He was attacked. Then he sees Antonio. Finding his friend alive fills Sebastian with joy.

Sebastian notices that everybody is staring at him in disbelief. Following Antonio's gaze, he spots what looks like his mirror image standing by Orsino. Both brother and sister are overcome with wonder. They question each other, trying to discover whether what they see is true.

NOTE: Notice again how cautious Viola and Sebastian are. Their behavior contrasts sharply with that of the characters who rashly believe anything they are told. In a play that exposes the types of foolishness people are liable to fall into, these two characters are sensible.

Finally, Viola and her brother admit what their hearts have told them since they first spied each other. Viola reveals to everybody who she really is. She explains that the sea captain who rescued her has her woman's clothing.

Sebastian jokes with Olivia, saying that she was almost betrothed to a girl, "But nature to her bias drew in that."

NOTE: Read that line again. It contains the key to unravelling the confusions of the play. He and Olivia were drawn together, Sebastian says, because that's how it should be in the natural order of things. Almost every character in the play tries to fool himself or others. In the end, the true nature of each one is revealed.

Orsino is overjoyed to find out Viola's true nature. He asks whether she meant it when she said she would never love any woman as she loved him. Viola affirms that she meant what she said.

NOTE: The Romantic Plot has now been resolved. The obstacles between the lovers melt away as the confusions are cleared up. To Shakespeare's audience, it would have seemed perfectly natural that the characters of noble birth should have been attracted to each other, even in disguise. According to the Elizabethan sense of order, God ordains your place in life. Orsino, Viola, Olivia, and Sebastian would thus be suited for each other and for no other characters in the play.

Viola cannot change into her women's clothes, because Malvolio had the sea captain put in jail for reasons Shakespeare never makes clear. Mention of Malvolio reminds Olivia that her steward seems to have lost his mind. Feste says that he has a letter from Malvolio. He begins to shout out the letter, imitating the way Malvolio spoke while locked in the dark cell.

Olivia orders Fabian to read the letter, instead. In it, Malvolio says that he was treated shamefully. He explains that he was only following the instructions in Olivia's own letter. Olivia concludes that he doesn't sound crazy. She orders him released and brought to her.

Now that Orsino and Olivia have their proper mates, peace can be made between them. Olivia offers to hold the weddings at her house and at her expense. Orsino accepts and promises Viola he will marry her. Olivia gladly accepts her former beloved as a sister.

Lines 349–415

Malvolio enters, shaking with rage. He says he has been wronged. To prove it, he shows Olivia the letter. She admits the handwriting looks like hers, but she recognizes it as Maria's. She sweetly apologizes to Malvolio and promises that he will be able to sit in judgment on whoever played the trick on him.

Fabian steps forward to confess his and Sir Toby's part in the joke. He doesn't want to mar the happiness of the day with any bad feelings. Sir Toby and he invented the joke to get even with Malvolio, he explains. Maria wrote the letter to please Sir Toby. In return, Sir Toby has married her.

They and Malvolio are now even, according to Fabian. He suggests that everybody should have a good laugh and forget about it. The fool agrees.

Malvolio cannot forgive his tormentors. Angrily vowing revenge on everybody, he stomps out.

NOTE: Unlike the others, Malvolio remains a victim of his vain self-deception to the end. His pride prevents him from laughing at himself. He can neither forgive nor accept forgiveness. Shakespeare seems to be saying that you can't avoid looking foolish at times. The only solution, according to the play, is to laugh and forgive.

Olivia feels sorry for Malvolio. Servants are sent to chase after the man and make peace with him. Orsino vows to remain in Olivia's house until the marriages take place.

NOTE: Shakespearean comedies end in marriage. Tragedies end in death. Thus, *Hamlet* concludes with a funeral procession, while *A Midsummer Night's Dream* ends with a wedding march.

Lines 416–435

The final moments of the play are Feste's. The fool closes the show with a song. The nature of his song is rather surprising. At the end of a comedy you might expect a light little "ditty." Instead, you get a melancholy ballad.

The lyrics concern the stages of a man's life—from boy to man to husband to bed-ridden old man. Images of rain and wind fill the verses.

"The rain it raineth every day" goes the refrain. That is not literally true. In fact, some readers consider the song mere nonsense verse. That could be true. But think about what the image of rain could signify. The refrain could mean "each day goes by and is washed away into the past." It could also mean "every day you have troubles."

Look at the final verse. It could speak for Shakespeare the playwright:

A long while ago the world began,
With hey, ho, the wind and the rain;
But that's all one, our play is done,
And we'll strive to please you every day.
                    (V, i, 432–435)

He may be saying: time goes on; people have troubles; everybody gets old and dies. All I can do is entertain you with my play. Remember it is a play in which the actors have been playing characters who in turn pretend to be what they are not. As a character in a different play says, "All the world's a stage."

As you've seen, *Twelfth Night* portrays a whole range of faults that humans fall prey to. It finally takes an amused, forgiving view of those faults in a song which reminds us of the sadness of life but says, "What can you do? Just laugh."

Is it possible that Shakespeare included it because the actor who played Feste sang it especially well? In that case, perhaps the verse *is* mere nonsense. Why do you think Shakespeare chose it to end his play? As with all questions of interpretation, you have to make your own choice.

A STEP BEYOND

Tests and Answers

TESTS

Test 1

1. Orsino's obsession with love is reflected in   _____
   his frequent desire
   A. to eat   B. to hear music
   C. to dance

2. In Acts I & II, Viola and Sebastian are both   _____
   sad because
   A. their father is dead
   B. they lost all their wealth in the
      shipwreck
   C. each thinks the other is dead

3. Sir Toby keeps Sir Andrew around because   _____
   A. they are old army friends
   B. Andrew makes him laugh
   C. Andrew lends him money

4. Maria makes a good match for Toby be-   _____
   cause they
    I. are equally clever
   II. both like mischief
   III. are both rich
       A. I only   B. I and II only
       C. I, II, and III

5. When Viola tells Orsino about the love "her   _____
   sister" had for a man, she's really talking
   about

A. her own love for Orsino
B. her mother's love for her father
C. Olivia's love for Cessario

6. Sir Andrew starts quarrels but never fights _____
   because
   A. he's too gentle at heart
   B. his reputation frightens his opponents
   C. he's a coward

7. Before he finds Maria's letter, Malvolio is _____
   A. thinking about marrying Olivia
   B. taking a ring to Cesario
   C. trading quips with Feste

8. When Toby asks Malvolio "Dost thou think, _____
   because thou art virtuous, there shall be no
   more cakes and ale?" he means
   A. just because you don't have fun
      doesn't mean others can't
   B. you should not expect virtue to
      overcome appetite
   C. cakes and ale cannot be equated

9. When Olivia first sees Sebastian, she _____
   A. has him arrested
   B. thinks he is Cesario
   C. is in disguise

10. Sir Toby and Sir Andrew are given "bloody _____
    coxcombs" by
    A. Orsino   B. Antonio
    C. Sebastian

11. Compare the social conditions of Shakespeare's
    London and *Twelfth Night*'s Illyria.

12. How do we know that Orsino is in love with love?

13. Why does Malvolio fall for Maria's practical joke?

14. What is Feste's function in the play?

15. What do we learn about the characters from the way they speak?

Test 2

1. The Sea Captain tells Viola that Orsino is _____
   A. an affectioned ass
   B. wise enough to play the fool
   C. a noble duke

2. Sir Andrew says he's going home because _____
   A. Olivia has no interest in him
   B. Toby hurt his feelings
   C. he's out of money

3. The first time Olivia meets Cesario, she _____
   A. falls in love with him
   B. knows he is a girl in disguise
   C. will not talk to him

4. Maria's letter instructs Malvolio to _____
   I. put on yellow stockings
   II. dance a jig
   III. smile constantly
      A. I and II only   B. II and III only
      C. I and III only

5. When Malvolio seems mad, Olivia says she _____
   A. may command where she adores
   B. cannot love him
   C. would not have him miscarry for the half of her dowry

6. Sir Andrew changes his mind about chal-   ____
   lenging Cesario because
   A. Sir Toby says Cesario is his cousin
   B. Sir Toby says Cesario is a very good
      swordsman
   C. Olivia forbids fighting

7. When Viola says her sister "let conceal-   ____
   ment, like a worm i' the bud,/ feed on her
   damask cheek," she's using a
     I. simile
    II. metaphor
    II. hyperbole
        A. I and II only   B. I and III only
        C. II and III only

8. Malvolio's attitude towards those who   ____
   played the joke on him is
   A. sarcastic   B. whimsical
   C. vengeful

9. Viola refuses Antonio's request for his purse   ____
   because
   A. she needs the money
   B. he never gave it to her
   C. she wants revenge on him

10. When Olivia wants to marry him, Sebas-   ____
    tian is
    A. amazed and delighted
    B. glad of the chance to get a rich wife
    C. shocked at the speed of her proposal

11. By comparing Feste and Sir Andrew, explore the
    different meanings of the word "fool."

12. Discuss the significance of disguise in *Twelfth Night*.

13. How are the Romantic Plot and the Low Comic Plot thematically unified?

14. Based on this play, what would you say was Shakespeare's attitude towards human foolishness?

15. What do you learn from the songs Feste sings?

ANSWERS

Test 1

1. B **2.** C **3.** C **4.** B **5.** A **6.** C
7. A **8.** A **9.** B **10.** C

11. Use the section of this book about "The Author and His Times" to help you. You could start by pointing out that in Illyria, as in Elizabethan England, you find a well-defined social order. Talk about what we learn about each class from the example of the characters as Shakespeare draws them.

Another parallel exists in the fact that, in Elizabethan England, social climbing was possible, but was not always considered admirable. Examine Sir Andrew's lack of skill in courtly virtues in the light of his wealth and the fact that, in Elizabethan England, it was possible to buy a title. It's especially profitable to look at Malvolio from the point of view of social climbing. Explore how the possibility of improving his status could both lead to his actions and explain why the others so dislike him. Show how Feste is free to move among the various levels of society, just as Elizabethan fools could.

You can also deal with the Romantic Plot in terms of the medieval ideal of Courtly Love as inherited by the Elizabethans. Orsino makes a good example. Show how his fixation with Olivia reflects the Courtly convention of the chaste lover.

Finally, you can point out how the resolution of *Twelfth Night* reaffirms the Elizabethan sense of order. Mention the fact that those who tried to rise above their "rightful station" are punished. Suitable partners are found for all the marriageable characters. A sense of balance is restored to Illyria.

12. Orsino's character description in this book will help you. You can also use the discussion of Romantic Love in the "themes" section.

Orsino says he is in love with Olivia. Do his words and actions support that claim? Which does he seem to want more—Olivia, or that sweet Romantic feeling that her rejection gives him? What about the fact that he stays home and sends messengers to do his talking for him? Do you believe he's really trying to win the lady's hand?

Discuss the content of Orsino's speeches. Note how often he speaks about love in the abstract and how relatively little he actually says about Olivia. Also examine Orsino's preoccupation with music. Pay special attention to the song Feste sings in Act II, Scene iv.

13. The chink in Malvolio's armor is his self-love, or vanity. Show how Maria's deception is shrewdly chosen from that point of view. Demonstrate how clearly Maria sees him by comparing what she says about him (*Act II, Scene iii*) with what we know about the man from observation. He does act like a Puritan when others are around. When he's alone in the garden, however, we learn that he's really only concerned with social status.

Self love makes Malvolio blind. If he had any objectivity, he would have to at least wonder about the letter's authenticity. His behavior the next time he sees Olivia (*Act III, Scene iv*) shocks the lady. Malvolio, however, is too self-absorbed to notice.

14. To answer this question, consider the function of an "allowed" fool. He was essentially an entertainer.

Clarify what Feste does and does not do. Feste never advances the plot. He takes part in the practical joke played on Malvolio, but it's not his idea. He never seems to *want* anything from the other characters except whatever money he can beg from them.

Therefore, Feste has a sense of perspective that the others lack. Cite several ways he helps to put the others and their actions into perspective. Look at his conversation with Olivia about her brother in Act I, Scene v. What do we learn about Sir Toby, Sir Andrew and Maria from the way he relates to them?

You might wish to comment on the way Feste resembles some modern-day comedians. Can you think of any entertainers who, while making us laugh, also give us insights into ourselves and our society?

15. Here you can talk about Shakespeare's use of language. Refer to this guide's discussion of style for help. Show how characters are revealed by the imagery they use. Orsino's love is excessive and indulgent. Therefore, his speech is filled with sensual images (food, flowers) and talk of death. Viola's love is simple and genuine. When she speaks of love, her statements are spare and poignant. (See Act I, Scene v, lines 273–281 and Act II, Scene iv, lines 125–133.) Find other examples.

Sometimes we can see the truth behind a misleading appearance by paying attention to the way the character uses language. One example would be Sir Toby. He may appear to be nothing more than a drunkard. When we look at how cleverly he uses words in his scenes with

Maria and Feste, we get a deeper insight into his character.

Test 2

1. C   **2.** A   **3.** A   **4.** C   **5.** C   **6.** B

7. A   **8.** C   **9.** B   **10.** A

11. As Feste points out in Act III, Scene i, words can have several meanings. "Fool" is no exception. To talk about the word as it applies to Feste, use the same approach as in answering question 14 of Test 1. Feste's "foolery" both entertains and instructs.

Andrew, on the other hand, fits a more literal definition of a fool. He is a simpleton, what the Elizabethans would call a "natural" fool. As Viola says, Feste must be keenly aware of everything going on around him. Andrew never quite knows what's going on. Feste's skill demands that he know several meanings for every word. Andrew has trouble following the drift of a simple conversation. Find more ways of contrasting the two. Support your statements with examples from the text.

12. You can talk about the significance of disguise from two points of view: 1) how it affects the plot, and 2) how it works thematically. Viola's disguise is a major plot device. Wearing her disguise, she comes into the middle of the impasse between Orsino and Olivia. When she removes her disguise, the conflict is resolved. Trace how the complications arise step by step as a consequence of her disguise. Incidental disguises, such as Feste's as Sir Topas, help to unify the various plots.

Thematically, the use of disguise reminds us that people are not always what they appear to be. Discuss the way Orsino "disguises" himself when he claims to be in love with Olivia. Malvolio and Andrew also attempt to disguise their true natures. You might discuss the way the latter two are even disguised from themselves, that is, they are self-deceived.

13. Both plots deal with the exposure of human folly. In the Romantic Plot, we see the mad behavior produced by the excesses of love. Discuss the types of foolishness exhibited by Orsino and Olivia. The Low Comic Plot deals mainly with the types of foolishness engendered by pride and vanity. Give examples.

Another theme that unifies the plots is the idea that love is madness. Pick several characters from each plot and show how their mad behavior is dictated by love (which can also mean *self*-love, remember). For example, you might talk about Olivia's love for Viola, Antonio's love for Sebastian, and Malvolio's love for himself, and how each behaves foolishly as a consequence.

14. From the evidence of this play, it appears that Shakespeare accepted and forgave human foolishness. He saw that everybody was driven to behave foolishly at times. Give an overview of the reasons people behave foolishly in *Twelfth Night*. Mention that even the noble characters are prone to foolishness. Still, Shakespeare did not excuse such behavior. He saw it as a problem that needed to be set right. In the end of the play, the fools are all exposed. The characters who see beyond their past foolishness are rewarded. Those who can't (Malvolio in particular) continue to suffer. So you could say that Shakespeare seemed to view foolishness as an unavoidable part of human existence. But he seemed to regard it as a forgivable sin.

15. Each of the songs relates specifically to a character, a set of characters or a theme. Use the sections of the scene-by-scene analysis that refer to the scenes in which each song appears.

In Act II, Scene iii, Feste sings two songs. The first, "O mistress mine, where are you roaming?" relates to the Romantic plot. Discuss how it does. Pay special attention to the line "Journeys end in lovers meeting" (that foreshadows the end of the play). The second song comments on the Low Comic characters.

In Act II, Scene iv, he sings "Come away death" at Orsino's request. Explore what this song tells us about Orsino's character. Viola also understands the feeling of the song. Tell why.

This book's analysis of the play's final scene examines Feste's last song in detail. Describe how the song helps to put the play in perspective.

Term Paper Ideas and other Topics for Writing

Disguise

1. Trace the effects of Viola's disguise throughout the play.

2. How does the fact that Malvolio presents himself to the world as a Puritan relate to his own self-deception?

3. In what way is the fool in disguise? Discuss the manner in which he disguises his wisdom as "foolery."

4. Contrast the way in which Viola disguises herself to others with the way Malvolio, Orsino and Sir Andrew deceive themselves.

5. Viola says that disguise is a wickedness. Is that how it functions in *Twelfth Night*?

Love

1. Identify four types of love in *Twelfth Night*. Discuss what the play has to say about each.

2. How does Viola's love for Orsino differ from Orsino's love for Olivia?

3. How does the concept of Romantic, Courtly Love affect the characters?

4. Write about *Twelfth Night* as an exploration of the madness of love.

5. Identify as many types of false love in the play as possible. Contrast each with Viola's true love.

Characters

1. How does Viola keep her balance despite her difficult situation?

2. Discuss the many sides of Olivia's personality we see in the play.

3. How does Feste interact with each of the other characters? What do we learn about each of those characters from Feste?

4. What makes Sir Toby Belch and Sir Andrew Aguecheek such a comic team?

5. Each of the characters who pair off in the end to be married is well-suited to his or her mate. In what way? How do we know that?

6. Does *Twelfth Night* have a central character, or is it equally concerned with several? If there is a central char-

acter, who is it? If there isn't, is there a central idea to which each character relates?

Style

1. How is the imagery of music developed throughout the play?

2. Using one of the following characters, show how Shakespeare uses language to reveal character:

Orsino
Sir Toby Belch
Viola
Malvolio

Plot

1. Identify as many separate plots as you can. Show how they are woven together.

2. Is *Twelfth Night* a unified play or an assembly of separate plots? Explain.

3. Explore whether any of the plot lines could exist without the others. Does each contain its own independent chain of causes and reactions?

4. How do the Romantic plot and the Low Comic plot reflect one another?

5. Shakespeare has to make several implausible plot twists seem believable. Identify three and show how, as a dramatist, he handles each.

Social Structure

1. Discuss the humiliation of Malvolio as the story of a social climber who gets his comeuppance.

2. Identify the levels of society in *Twelfth Night*. Explore in what ways they are similar to each other and in what ways they differ.

3. In what ways does the action of *Twelfth Night* temporarily turn the social order topsy-turvey?

4. How does Feste fit into the social structure of the play?

Further Reading
CRITICAL WORKS

Barber, Cesar Lombardi. *Shakespeare's Festive Comedy*. Princeton, N.J.: Princeton University Press, 1959.

Barton, Anne. "*As You Like It* and *Twelfth Night*: Shakespeare's Sense of an Ending," in *Shakespearean Comedy*. London: Edward Arnold, 1972.

Berman, Ronald. *A Reader's Guide to Shakespeare's Plays*. Glenview, Illinois: Scott, Foresman, 1973.

Brown, John Russell. *Shakespeare's Plays in Performance*. New York: St. Martin's Press, 1967.

Draper, John William. *The* Twelfth Night *of Shakespeare's Audience*. Stanford: Stanford University Press, 1950. Analysis of *Twelfth Night* in terms of Elizabethan social codes.

Evans, Bertrand. *Shakespeare's Comedies*. Oxford: Clarendon Press, 1969. Detailed structural analysis of *Twelfth Night*.

Goldsmith, Robert Hollis. *Wise Fools in Shakespeare*. Michigan: Michigan State University Press, 1955. An exploration of the nature of the fool's skill.

Hazlitt, William. *Characters of Shakespeare's Plays*. London: Oxford University Press, 1970. A classic study of Shakespeare, first published in 1817.

Hotson, Leslie. *The First Night of* Twelfth Night. London: R. Hart-Davis, 1954. Speculates that the play was first performed for Queen Elizabeth at court, and interprets the play as topical satire.

Kantak, V. Y. "An Approach to Shakespearean Comedy." *Shakespeare Survey* 22(1974):7–14.

King, Walter N., ed. *Twentieth Century Interpretations of Twelfth Night*. Englewood Cliffs, N.J.: Prentice Hall, Inc.,1968. A collection of essays about the play.

Knight, Charles. *Studies of Shakespeare*. New York: AMS Press, Inc., 1971. Reprint of a guide to Shakespeare's works first published in 1849.

Nagarajan, S. "What You Will," in *the Shakespeare Quarterly* Vol. X (1959):61–67. Examines the theme of the difference between what we are and what we desire.

Salingar, Leo. "The Design of *Twelfth Night*," in *The Shakespeare Quarterly* Vol. IX (1958):117–139. A very good introduction to the play.

Salingar, Leo. *Shakespeare and the Traditions of Comedy*. London: Cambridge University Press, 1974.

Summers, Joseph H. "The Masks of *Twelfth Night*," in *University Review* XXII (1955):25–32. Explores the theme of disguise.

Van Doren, Mark. *Shakespeare*. New York: H. Holt and Company, 1939.

Welsford, Enid. *The Fool; His Social and Literary History*. London: Farber and Farber, 1935. Tells the history of traditional Twelfth Night revels.

AUTHOR'S WORKS

Shakespeare wrote 37 plays (38 if you include *The Two Noble Kinsmen*) over a 20-year period, from about 1590 to 1610. It's difficult to determine the exact dates when many were written, but scholars

have made the following intelligent guesses about
his plays and poems:

Plays

1588–93	*The Comedy of Errors*
1588–94	*Love's Labor's Lost*
1590–91	*2 Henry VI*
1590–91	*3 Henry VI*
1591–92	*1 Henry VI*
1592–93	*Richard III*
1592–94	*Titus Andronicus*
1593–94	*The Taming of the Shrew*
1593–95	*The Two Gentlemen of Verona*
1595	*Richard II*
1594–96	*A Midsummer Night's Dream*
1596–97	*King John*
1596–97	*The Merchant of Venice*
1597	*1 Henry IV*
1597–98	*2 Henry IV*
1598–1600	*Much Ado About Nothing*
1598–99	*Henry V*
1599	*Julius Caesar*
1599–1600	*As You Like It*
1599–1600	*Twelfth Night*
1600–01	*Hamlet*
1597–1601	*The Merry Wives of Windsor*
1601–02	*Troilus and Cressida*
1602–04	*All's Well That Ends Well*
1603–04	*Othello*
1604	*Measure for Measure*
1605–06	*King Lear*
1605–06	*Macbeth*
1606–07	*Antony and Cleopatra*
1605–08	*Timon of Athens*
1607–09	*Coriolanus*

Glossary

Aqua-vitae Liquor.

Arion An ancient poet who jumped ship to avoid being murdered by his crew; he was rescued by a dolphin.

Belzebub The devil.

Canary A sweet wine from the Canary Islands.

Collier Coal seller.

Coranto A dance with quick steps.

Cuckold Someone whose wife deceives him with another man.

Damask Blended red and white.

Elysium Heaven.

Eunuch A castrated boy, valued for his soprano voice.

Fadge Succeed.

Galliard A lively dance.

Gaskins Hose.

Lethe The river of forgetfulness in Hades.

Mercury A god noted for trickiness.

Motley Particolored garb of a court fool.

Nuncio Messenger.

Penthesilea Queen of the Amazons.

'**Slid**   God's eyelid.
Sophy   Shah of Persia.
Viol de gamboys   A bass viol.

The Critics

On Shakespeare's Point of View in *Twelfth Night*

Folly is indigenous to the soil, and shoots out with native, happy, unchecked luxuriance. Absurdity has every encouragement afforded it; and nonsense has room to flourish in. Nothing is stunted by the churlish, icy hand of indifference or severity. The poet runs riot in conceit, and idolizes a quibble. His whole object is to turn the meanest or rudest objects to a pleasurable account. The relish which he has of a pun, or of the quaint humour of a low character, does not interfere with the delight with which he describes a beautiful image, or the most refined love. The clown's forced jests do not spoil the sweetness of the character of Viola; the same house is big enough to hold Malvolio, the Countess, Maria, Sir Toby, and Sir Andrew Aguecheek.

> *William Hazlitt*, Characters of
> Shakespeare's Plays, *1817*

On Disguise

Every character has his mask, for the assumption of the play is that no one is without a mask in the seriocomic business of the pursuit of happiness. The character without disguises who is not ridiculous is outside the realm of comedy. Within comedy, the character who thinks it is possible to live without assuming a mask is merely too naïve to recognize the mask he has already assumed. He is the chief object of laughter. As a general rule, we laugh with the characters who know the role they are playing and we laugh at those who do not; we can crudely

divide the cast of *Twelfth Night* into those two cat-
egories.

> *Joseph H. Summers*, The Masks of
> *Twelfth Night*, 1955

On Being in Love with Love

At the opening of the play Orsino and Olivia accept
the aristocratic (and literary) ideas of the romantic
lover and the grief stricken lady as realities rather
than ideas. They are comic characters exactly because of that confusion. Orsino glories in the proper
moodiness and fickleness of the literary lover; only
our own romanticism can blind us to the absurdities
in his opening speech. . . . Orsino is a victim of a
type of madness to which the most admirable characters are sometimes subject. Its usual causes are
boredom, lack of physical love, and excessive imagination, and the victim is unaware that he is in love
with love rather than with a person.

> *Joseph H. Summers*, The Masks of
> *Twelfth Night*, 1955

On Feste

There is only one character [Feste] who can restore
some sense of unity to *Twelfth Night* at its ending,
mediating between the world of the romantic lovers
and our own world, which is (or is about to be) that
of the chastened Sir Andrew, the sobered Belch and
the unbending Malvolio. In a sense, he has been
doing just this all along in preparation for some
such ultimate necessity. Throughout *Twelfth Night*,
Feste has served as commentator and Chorus,
mocking the extravagance of Orsino, the wasteful
idealism of Olivia's grief, Viola's poor showing as a
man. He has joined in the revels of Sir Toby and
Sir Andrew while remaining essentially apart from
them, aware of their limitations.

> *Anne Barton*, As You Like It and
> *Twelfth Night*: Shakespeare's
> Sense of an Ending, 1972

On Olivia

Indeed, Olivia gives evidence of a clear head and a quick mind. She enjoys the combat of wits between Malvolio and Feste; and, though she is too dignified in her mourning to make one in it, she eggs on the contestants. She is competent at worldly-wise epigram:"O world, how apt the poor are to be proud?"; and ". . . youth is bought more oft then begg'd, or borrow'd." She is quick-witted, and instantly invents the stratagem of the ring to oblige Viola to visit her again. She can endure plain speaking, and is not angry when Viola suggests that her fine complexion may be false and that she is "too proud." She can be patient with Feste, and can bide her time with Sir Toby. Indeed, she has poise and self-control.

John W. Draper, The *Twelfth Night* of Shakespeare's Audience, *1950*

Two Views of Malvolio

He is of a new order—ambitious, self-contained, cold and intelligent, and dreadfully likely to prevail. That is why Sir Toby and his retinue hate him. Feste at the end provides too simple an explanation. The humiliation of Malvolio, he says, was his personal revenge upon one who had discounted him to his mistress as "a barren rascal," a jester unworthy of hire. But the others had been as active as Feste, and they had had no such motive. "The devil a puritan that he is," Maria insists, "or anything constantly, but a time-pleaser; and affection'd ass." Puritan or not, Malvolio has offended them as a class. They could have forgiven his being a climber, his having affection for himself, if he had been any other kind of man than the cool kind he is.

Mark Van Doren, Shakespeare, *1939*

Malvolio is to our minds as poetical as Don Quixote; and we are by no means sure that Shakespeare meant the poor cross-gartered steward *only* to be laughed at, any more than Cervantes did the knight of the rueful countenance. He meant us to pity him, as Olivia and the Duke pitied him; for, in truth, the delusion by which Malvolio was wrecked, only passed out of the romantic into the comic through the manifestation of the vanity of the character in reference to his situation. But if we laugh at Malvolio we are not to laugh ill-naturedly, for the poet has conducted all the mischief against him in a spirit in which there is no real malice at the bottom of the fun.

Charles Knight, Studies of
Shakespeare, *1849*